Paris Boulangerie-Pâtisserie

Paris Boulangerie-Pâtisserie

BY LINDA DANNENBERG

PHOTOGRAPHS BY

GUY BOUCHET

CLARKSON POTTER/PUBLISHERS

NEW YORK

DESIGN ASSISTANT: LEAH LOCOCO

LIBRARY OF CONGRESS CATALOGING-IN-PUBLICATION DATA

DANNENBERG, LINDA.
    PARIS BOULANGERIE-PÀTISSERIE / BY LINDA DANNENBERG — 1ST ED.
    INCLUDES INDEX.
    1. BAKING. 2. COOKERY, FRENCH. 3. BAKERS AND BAKERIES—FRANCE—PARIS—GUIDEBOOKS. 4. PARIS (FRANCE)—GUIDEBOOKS. I. TITLE. TX765.D26 1994 641.7'1—DC20
                                                                                93-36414

ISBN 0-517-59221-5

10 9 8 7 6 5 4 3

For Steve and for Benjamin, who make my life so sweet

ll in the name of research, I roamed the streets of Paris, sampling *croissants aux amandes, tartes aux pommes,* baguettes crisp and golden, *gâteaux au chocolat, kugelhopfs, pains aux raisins, charlottes aux framboises, cakes aux fruits* and myriad other baked *délices* from *pâtisseries* and *boulangeries* large and small, antique and sparklingly modern. I took notes that filled four large notebooks, and made lists and more lists of properties and their wares, revising and updating constantly, eventually arriving at a short list of under twenty bakeries and a substantially longer one of about one hundred breads and pastries. Finally came the moment to confront the most crucial question of the project, the answer to which would determine the existence, or nonexistence, of this book: Would the bakers of Paris, a notoriously competitive and individualistic bunch, reveal their recipes for publication? They would and they did. Some required just a bit more coaxing and perseverance than others, but in the end my baker's dozen of world-class *pâtissiers* and *boulangers* showed immense generosity of spirit in sharing their time, their thoughts, and their trade secrets. It is to these men, and three remarkable women, that I owe my deepest gratitude:

Bernard, Valérie, and Isabelle Ganachaud; Basile Kamir; Jean-Luc Poujauran; André Lerch; Max Poilâne; Nadine Bernardé, Pascal Niau, and Michel Baglan; Gaston Lenôtre; Gérard Mulot; Jean-Marie Desfontaines; Robert Linxe; Pierre Lienard, François Duthu, and Claude Moreau; Marcel Haupois; and Jean-Michel Noël and Henri Grenier.

I am also grateful to two Paris friends, Françoise Ledoux-Wernert and Isabelle Pilate, who were especially helpful and supportive during this project. Thanks, too, to Pierre Hussenot, a wonderful photographer and colleague, for introducing me to the temptations of Au Péché Mignon. I would also like to express my thanks to Patrick Trautmann, for sharing some memories of his Paris childhood, and to Nivès Falcioni for taking me along twenty years ago to the first little shop of Gérard Mulot for a taste of his addictive macarons.

To my great good friends Pierre Moulin and Pierre LeVec, my heartfelt appreciation for often letting me make their Paris pied-à-terre my home-away-from-home while I worked on this book. And, as always, I would like to thank my wonderful agents, Gayle Benderoff and Deborah Geltman, who shepherd my ideas and proposals from dream to reality with such aplomb.

For his invaluable culinary expertise and advice and his superbly professional recipe testing, I am deeply grateful to Richard Sax; also to his colleagues, Nick Malgieri, pastry chef *par excellence,* Luli Gray, and Sandy Gluck.

My books would be very different entities without the glorious and evocative photographs of my longtime friend and photographer, Guy Bouchet. I am full of wonder in contemplating a lively and always fresh collaboration that has spanned continents and is now in its second decade. I am also most grateful to the awesomely talented Louise Fili whose sensitive and lovely design for this book captures the essence of the traditional French *pâtisserie* and conveys the spirit of Vieux Paris; thanks, too, to her terrific assistant, Leah Lococo.

Finally, I want to thank all of my colleagues at Clarkson Potter/Publishers who work so hard and are so very good at what they do: Katie Workman, Lauren Shakely, Howard Klein, Barbara Marks, Phyllis Fleiss, Janet McDonald, Mark McCauslin, Joan Denman, and Renato Stanisic. They consistently produce some of the most beautiful books I've seen anywhere, and I am proud to have such a fruitful and long-term association with this distinguished house.

DECORATIVE ANTIQUE PANELS, WITH PAINTED CANVAS UNDER GLASS, STILL ADORN MANY PARIS BAKERIES.

"The croissants taste like they were made by angels; the coffee tastes like it was concocted by the devil," my father wrote home on one of his first trips to Paris in the early 1950s. On subsequent trips he grew to love the strong, intense French coffees—*au lait* in the morning, *un express* after lunch and dinner—almost as much as the brioches, the *chausson aux pommes,* the *pain au chocolat,* the *savarins,* and the other celestial *pâtisserie* he discovered during his Gallic sojourns. On my own first day in Paris, during the long, hot summer of 1968, I went straight to a *pâtisserie-boulangerie* to buy a true French croissant—the classic, the cliché of French pastry. Once inside, I was overwhelmed by the incredible, seductive aromas and the amazing array of pastries and breads in one little shop. I ended up toting brioches, quiches Lorraines, *millefeuilles, saucissons en croûte, tartelettes aux fraises,* and a baguette, in addition to the requisite croissants, back to my little dormitory room where I feasted in lonely splendor for two days.

Self-control tends to evaporate in a Paris *pâtisserie-boulangerie;* the enticements to eyes, nose, and mouth are simply too powerful to resist. The shops themselves are beguiling, many endowed with lavish Belle Epoque detailing—ornate moldings, romantic painted glass panels, cherubs running rampant—and dazzling with the sparkle of gemlike *pâtisseries* set on white or gold paper doilies and displayed, like a Van Cleef tiara, each on a pedestal and individually lit. These havens of sweetness and light, where all is beautiful, delicious, and immediately available for instant gratification, are among the many traditional pleasures that make Paris so alluring.

Every Parisian I know harbors fond childhood memories involving the *pâtisserie-boulangerie.* One friend of mine recalls long *métro* rides on Sunday mornings with Papa or *Grand-père,* taken to bring back the perfect *tarte aux fruits rouges* or a *charlotte aux poires* from an out-of-the-way *pâtisserie* for the family dinner; another speaks warmly of the *boulangerie* across from his *lycée,* where big, buttery croissants would always come out of the oven three minutes after the morning bell rang, generating a daily mound of tardy slips. The *pâtisserie-boulangerie* is a happy part of every Parisian's life, and these beloved institutions are ubiquitous. The golden glow of glazed brioches and gilded mirrors that suffuses the bakeries of Paris lights up almost every block throughout the city. At first glance, the wonder is that so many of them thrive. Yet, knowing Paris well provides the answer. You wouldn't suspect it from looking at the sleek passersby rushing along one of the *grands boulevards* or strolling along the elegant streets of the sixteenth arrondissement, but this is a city with a sweet tooth, an enclave of soigné gourmands. For many Parisians their local *pâtisserie* offers a daily, discreet indulgence, a ten-minute escape from the office to nab their favorite little sweet. Perhaps it is a *brioche aux gouttes de chocolat,* a chocolate chip brioche, from Gérard Mulot, or a *macaron au café,* a coffee macaroon, from Ladurée; a lemony madeleine from André Lerch, or an individual *tarte aux fraises* from Dalloyau. Nobody has to answer for this lovely, licit pleasure.

These days, most of the bakeries in Paris are *pâtisseries-boulangeries,* indicating that they offer both pastries and breads. Some exclusive *pâtisseries,* such as Stohrer and Ladurée, still exist, but most bakers, despite more extensive training in and a proclivity toward one specialty or the other, are proficient in the two disciplines. The *pâtissiers* offer a few simple breads so that their customers can do one-stop shopping for their baked goods, while the boulangers offer the rustic, home-style *"gâteaux boulangers,"* or baker's pastries, that are much less complex in concept and preparation than the elaborate confections of the *pâtissier*'s art. But this melding of disciplines wasn't always so. Up until the 1800s, you were one or the other, either a *boulanger* or a *pâtissier,* not both. The *boulangers* hated the idea of working with butter and sugar, the greasiness and stickiness anathema to their sensibilities. (A few top bakers today still express this sentiment.) They much preferred the purity of working with their doughs of flour, water, yeast, and salt. The *pâtissiers,* for their part, disdained the drudgery of the *boulangers,* the long, hard kneading (in the Dark Ages of French *boulange,* around the era of Charlemagne, the doughs from some flours, such as barley and oats, were so leaden and stiff they could only be kneaded with the feet), the intense heat of the *fournil,* or baking den, and the lack of variety and artistic skill in the baked goods. In fact, during the Middle Ages, there were actually two separate baking guilds—one for *boulangers* and one for *pâtissiers*—and there were occasionally intense squabbles about items that straddled the two categories. Meat pies, for example, were a bone of contention, since both groups claimed the right to produce them.

Public *boulangeries* have existed in Paris since the middle of the eighth century, when King Pépin le Bref, Pippin the Short, recognized bread baking as a trade. It was not until many centuries later, after the French Revolution, that the *pâtisseries* came into their own. When Marie Antoinette uttered her famous revolutionary, and oft misquoted, statement, *"Ils n'ont plus de pain, qu'ils mangent de la brioche"*—"They have no more bread, let them eat brioche"—she altered more than the course of French political history. With

André Lerch's cinnamon shortbread cookies are an Alsatian specialty.

OUTSIDE A RIGHT BANK BAKERY, A BROTHER AND SISTER STOP FOR A BAGUETTE AFTER SCHOOL.

the brutal downfall of the monarchy and its dependent aristocracy, many elite chefs and *pâtissiers* who had formerly been employed by the court or wealthy noble families suddenly found themselves booted out of the châteaux with no more princely bosses and no more work. What else to do but to open a *pâtisserie* shop in Paris where a sophisticated clientele of newly equal *citoyens* awaited their confections. Two pastry shops founded by chefs formerly employed by the aristocracy—Stohrer and Dalloyau—are still flourishing.

In the early nineteenth century, Marie-Antoine Carême, the brilliant pastry chef with an architectural avocation, was employed consecutively by the diplomat Talleyrand, Czar Alexander I, and England's George IV. He brought pastry making to the pinnacle of high art—figuratively and literally. With his elaborate, soaring architectural pastries, such as ornately decorated *pièces montées*—four- or five-foot-tall creations comprised of tiny *choux*, or cream puffs—and his many books on *pâtisserie,* the métier of pastry making made a quantum leap forward.

The métier of bread baking also evolved significantly during the same era. During the years Carême was designing and constructing his lavish confections, a coterie of Viennese bakers had migrated to Paris, opening a number of small *boulangeries* specializing in Austrian-style breads—usually made with milk, sugar, and butter. They also offered most of the items now typically associated with the French breakfast—croissants, Marie Antoinette's brioches (she was, of course, an Austrian princess before becoming a French queen), and *pains aux raisins*—which were soon adopted by both French *pâtissiers* and *boulangers* as part of their repertoire. These particular breakfast specialties are sometimes referred to as *"viennoiserie"*—pastries with Viennese origins. The Austrian bakers also baked a long, wandlike bread made of white flour, milk, yeast, salt, water, and butter. The bread was mostly crust with very little *mie,* or crumb, and customers found it pleasing. One theory on the origin of the classic French baguette links it directly to the introduction of the *pain Viennois* in Paris.

Paris today boasts the best bakers in France, drawn to the capital from provinces throughout the country. They have risen to the top and prospered, the crème de la crème in a competitive and unforgiving field. The variety of goods available within the city's twenty arrondissements is mind-boggling; the quality is incomparable. The competition among the *pâtissiers* and *boulangers* keeps them finely honed, the best always seeking to be better. Individuality is the key to success.

The *pâtissier* is an artist who wants his creations to be as individual as he is—which is the reason there are so many variations on a theme in the pastry shops of Paris, appealing to a broad range of Parisian tastes. Gourmands can argue endlessly about the relative merits of the pistachio *macarons* produced by Gérard Mulot, Ladurée, and Dalloyau; or debate the superiority of rustic apple tarts from Ganachaud, Max Poilâne, and the Moulin de la Vierge; even delve into the subtleties that distinguish the Mocambo, the Gounod, and the Pleyel, three intensely rich chocolate cakes by Robert Linxe of the Maison du Chocolat.

The top *boulangers* of Paris are a dedicated and idealistic bunch of artisans committed to the concept of old-fashioned, handmade breads, the kind of breads everyone took for granted in the years preceding World War II, before industrialization spread to bread baking in a major way. Commercially produced breads, widely available in supermarkets, slowly and insidiously undermined the palates of consumers, these bakers believe, "industrializing" the taste buds and dulling the memory for the way great breads should taste. Bakers like Bernard Ganachaud, Jean-Luc Poujauran, and Max and Lionel Poilâne have worked to recapture the *"pain d'autrefois"*—the breads of yesteryear—intensely flavored, wonderfully textured, with crisp, crackling crusts and tender hearts.

Walk into any good Paris *boulangerie* and you are confronted with an astonishing variety of just-baked breads: the baguette, of white flour, water, and yeast, and its cousins, the *ficelle*, skinny like a flute, the *bâtard*, short and stumpy, *au levain*, of sourdough, the *couronne*, shaped like a wreath, and the *galette*, squashed flat and round like a discus; *pain complet*, whole wheat bread; *pain de seigle*, rye bread, often offered *"aux raisins,"* with raisins; *pain de mie*, a traditional white sandwich loaf with fine texture and a thin, soft crust; *pain de son*, a dietetic bran bread; *pain au maïs*, a small rectangular loaf of corn bread; *pain de campagne*, "country bread" that varies from *boulanger* to *boulanger*, a hearty crusty loaf usually with a blend of flours—white and whole wheat, sometimes a bit of rye, formed in many shapes, but frequently a big, round *miche* or long ovoid loaf; *pain Viennois*, a sweet, baguette-shaped bread, made with powdered milk and sugar along with the white flour, water, and yeast; *pain aux noix* or *pain aux olives*, dense rye or wheat breads filled with walnuts or olives; *pain aux levain*, a classic, dense, sourdough loaf sometimes large enough to put your arms around; *fougasse*, a long, flat, lacy, "cutwork" bread usually of baguette dough, often ladder-shaped or tree-shaped and flavored with herbs, anchovies, bacon, onion, or cheese; and many more. With quality and choice comes price. Bread is becoming more expensive and more "upscale," with the best bakers buying organic flours that have been specially milled for them and then giving their doughs the luxury of time with very long fermentations. Many *boulangers* have become such purists that they refuse to sell any jams, jellies, or honeys with chemical additives alongside their organic, artisanal breads.

Passion and *passionate* are words frequently used in conversation on the subject of *boulangerie*, especially by the bakers themselves and those who have observed them closely. Great *boulangerie* is indeed a passion, and the best bakers working in the artisanal tradition give themselves to their work passionately, mentally and physically. Enthralled by the subject, any one of them can talk for hours on the magical transformation of the grain of wheat as it becomes bread, on the biochemical processes of fermentation, and on the nutritional value of any handmade loaf. But the concept of passion in *boulangerie* doesn't end with the warm and crusty loaf. Given the nature of the work and the nature of the French, passion in this métier almost inevitably takes on sexual overtones. "*C'est un travail très sensuel*—it's a very sensual kind of work," says Basile Kamir of the Moulin de la Vierge. "There's the heat of the *fournil*, so bakers are scantily dressed . . . and there's all the work with the hands massaging the dough; everything is done by touch. . . ." In the baker's world there are all kinds of ribald stories involving the *boulanger*, the *boulanger*'s wife—La Boulangère—and the pastry maker. You see, the baker worked at night and would take an afternoon siesta, either at home or in a local *maison* of ill-repute; meanwhile, the baker's wife was in the shop with the pastry maker, who worked during the day. . . . All apocryphal, of course. One famous Paris baker has a well-known collection of erotic art. Another likes to claim he was "*conçu sur le pétrin*"—conceived on the kneading table.

As with my first book in this genre, *Paris Bistro Cooking*, I have fashioned *Paris Boulangerie-Pâtisserie* to be as much a book of record as a cookbook, to capture the traditions, the wares, and the ambience of Paris bakeries as they exist today. While *pâtisseries* and *boulangeries* will probably never disappear from the face of Paris, many beautiful old shops have gone the way of many handsome, antique bistros—converted into boutiques or demolished to make way for a modern high rise. This kind of gentrification, although widely prevalent now in Paris, is hardly anything new, as Colette attests in *The Blue Lantern*, a journal written in the 1940s:

Next door to the "Boeuf" (a departed bistro), let a tear be shed for the Pâtisserie Flammang, *famed for its* éclairs *and Neapolitan ices, and*

A BEAUTIFUL TURN-OF-THE-CENTURY BOULANGERIE ON THE RIGHT BANK IS TODAY A FASHIONABLE CLOTHING BOUTIQUE.

for the departed glories of its glass panelling of the Restoration period, painted with garlands. The Flammangs were reduced to penury by selling their delicious cream-tarts and puff-pastries which simply ran away with the best butter.

I mourn the loss of the good proprietors themselves as much as that of their good confectionary. All among the flowered panels, as pleasing to the eye as those of the Grand Véfour, lived a family of ladies in black, the eldest of whom took her place at the desk. A younger sister supervised the faultless service of the waitresses, while a second generation, represented by a young woman of unobtrusive coloring, enquired after the health of the customers as she wrapped up a tartlet, a saint-honoré, *or a* savarin— *"Deliciously moist, is it not, Madame?"—in its conical tent of tissue-paper. A little girl who never opened her mouth made out fair copies of the bills close beside the cash desk. Flammang's is a co-op painted in bright green. The ravishing glass panels have found their way to the Carnavalet Museum. A fat lot of good that will do us—and them!*

The recipes I've collected in these pages, which I hope will transport you to Paris *en esprit*, come straight from the Paris *pâtissiers* and *boulangers*, formulated by them for the home cook. Many of the featured pastries and breads are classics, with each *pâtissier*'s or *boulanger*'s individual spin; others are innovative, unusual in concept and unique to the *pâtissier* or *boulanger* who developed them. As I prepare this book, and stare dreamily at Guy Bouchet's evocative photographs, the aromas, the sounds, the images, and especially the tastes of the Paris bakeries where I spent so much time come flooding back. For me, this has been a project to savor, from its conception several years ago while standing at the counter of a *pâtisserie* on the Avenue de Suffren, through the very pleasant research, tastings, and interviews, and finally to the recipe testing and writing. Each recipe, each bite of bread, tart, or cake, evokes for me its own special memory. I think often of Marcel Proust, delicately dipping his madeleine into a steaming cup of lime-blossom tea and, on tasting the pastry, being suddenly overwhelmed by the memories of a childhood sojourn in Normandy. Taste can indeed trigger transcendent experience. For Proust it was a return to Cabourg. For me, it is always back to Paris—early on a luminous morning . . . in the middle of a chill, windy afternoon . . . at the close of a romantic, lavender-tinged dusk—back to a city that long ago captured my heart.

L'Ancienne
Tradition

STOHRER

LADURÉE

DALLOYAU

DOMINATING STOHRER IS THIS ELEGANT GLASS MURAL ENTITLED LA RENOMÉE, PAINTED BY PAUL BAUDRY IN 1864.

Cake aux Olives et Jambon · Bombes Amandés

....

Mousse au Caramel et aux Poires

....

Tarte à la Rhubarbe · Fraisier

....

Pâté aux Trois Viandes en Croûte

Stohrer is part of the rich patrimony of Paris, the oldest *pâtisserie* in the city, and an officially designated *monument historique*. It was founded by the *pâtissier* Stohrer, a gifted and innovative chef originally from the French province of Lorraine. Stohrer made his name early in his culinary career as the personal *pâtissier* to Queen Marie, the Polish princess who married Louis XV in 1725. Obviously a true gourmand, Queen Marie had Stohrer follow her to Versailles, where he was the court's premier pastry chef for five years, producing lavish *pâtisseries* for the king and his retinue until he left to open his own shop in Paris, on the cobbled rue Montorgueil where it still stands.

In the mid-1980s, after a succession of owners over two centuries, the Stohrer enterprise was purchased by a young businessman and lawyer, Pierre Lienard, and his partner, chef François Duthu, formerly with the Hotel Méridien in Paris. Lienard and Duthu gave this venerable property, whose luster had diminished over the years, a new lease on life. Today, with its staff of thirty, Stohrer basks in its renaissance as a top *pâtisserie* and in its growing reputation as a prime caterer. The chief pastry chef in the house, Claude Moreau, works with his assistants in the same kitchen space where the original chef Stohrer prepared his cakes for the Paris aristocracy, and where, according to Moreau, all the counters and work tables were too low "because bakers used to

CHEF CLAUDE MOREAU, LEFT, AND
OWNERS PIERRE LIENARD AND
FRANÇOIS DUTHU, CENTER AND RIGHT,
TAKE A SHORT BREAK IN FRONT
OF THEIR SHOP.

. . . .

be shorter in earlier days." The *labo-ratoire*—Moreau's pastry kitchen—turns out beautiful, classic *pâtisseries* —such as the *Fraisier*, a strawberries-and-cream cake; the pear charlotte; and the *Mousse au Caramel et aux Poires*, a caramel-pear mousse cake—that gleam with a mirror-perfect *glaçage*, or glaze, it takes years to perfect. His *Bombes Amandés*, lemony domed tea cakes, are usually lined up like little soldiers across the countertops, giving off their irresistible almond-scented fragrance from three feet away. Chef Moreau's savory pastries are every bit as enticing as his sweet confections, particularly the *Cake aux Olives et Jambon*, a golden tea bread studded with olives and ham, and a delicious three-meat pâté enveloped in a rich and flaky pastry crust.

Chef Moreau's creations are displayed to advantage in Stohrer's beautiful surroundings. The decor of the shop dates from the mid-1800s, when painter Paul Baudry, whose murals adorn the walls of the Palais

Garnier, the old Paris Opera House, was commissioned to embellish Stohrer's interior. Baudry's gauzily clad nymphets, their hands full of wheat sheaves and *pâtisseries*, beam down from the walls, beneath a celestial trompe l'oeil painted ceiling featuring flowers and sky. Ornate, cream-colored moldings, large mirrors, and gilt trim all contribute to the sensation of walking into a large jewel box, where the ruby-, amber-, and citrine-toned pastries are themselves the gems.

❋

Cake aux Olives et Jambon

. . . .

[OLIVE AND HAM LOAF]

. . . .

2 CUPS LESS 2 TABLESPOONS/
240 G ALL-PURPOSE FLOUR

2 1/2 TEASPOONS BAKING POWDER

1/2 CUP/125 ML DRY WHITE WINE

1/2 CUP/125 ML DRY VERMOUTH

4 LARGE EGGS, BEATEN

7/8 CUP/200 ML MILD-FLAVORED
OLIVE OIL

. . . .

STOHRER HAS BECKONED TO PASSERS-
BY ON THE LIVELY RUE MONTORGUEIL
FOR MORE THAN 200 YEARS.

1 1/2 CUPS/200 G FINELY DICED
COOKED HAM

1 1/2 CUPS/150 G GRATED
GRUYÈRE CHEESE

1 1/4 CUPS/200 G GREEN OLIVES,
PITTED AND CHOPPED COARSE

Preheat the oven to 350°F./175°C. Sift the flour with the baking powder into a large mixing bowl or the bowl of an electric mixer. Make a well in the center; add the wine, vermouth, and eggs. Mix gently just until incorporated. Add the olive oil a few spoonfuls at a time, mixing until you have a smooth dough. Add the ham, cheese, and olives, mixing just until incorporated.

Grease an 8 x 4-inch/20 x 10-cm loaf pan; scrape in the batter. Bake until the loaf is golden brown and a toothpick inserted in the center emerges clean, about 55 minutes. Cool briefly on a wire rack; then invert the loaf onto the rack and cool completely.

MAKES 1 LOAF, SIX SERVINGS

❋

Bombes Amandés

. . . .

[LEMON-ALMOND CAKES]

. . . .

Claude Moreau makes these little rounded cakes in *oeufs en gelée* molds, which are oval metal molds. They work equally well in large (3-inch/8-cm) muffin tins. The fondant used to make the lemon paste can be bought at a confectioner's or bakery, or it can be mail-ordered (page 00). However, this recipe uses a minuscule amount, and the bombes work fine without the fondant.

PÂTE SUCRÉE

1/2 CUP (1 STICK) PLUS
2 TABLESPOONS/150 G COLD
UNSALTED BUTTER, CUT
INTO PIECES

3/8 TEASPOON SALT

1/3 CUP/30 G GROUND
BLANCHED ALMONDS

1 3/4 CUPS/225 G ALL-PURPOSE
FLOUR

3/4 CUP PLUS 2 TABLESPOONS/
120 G CONFECTIONERS' SUGAR

1 LARGE EGG

. . . .

on a lightly floured work surface to a thickness of about ⅛ inch/⅓ cm. Fit the pastry without stretching into the pan, forming an even edge about 2 inches/5 cm high up the sides of the springform pan. Patch any cracks with dough trimmings. Chill the pastry for ½ hour.

Preheat the oven to 375°F./190°C. Place the springform pan in a jelly roll pan or baking sheet. Line the pastry shell with parchment paper or lightly buttered aluminum foil and fill with dried beans or rice. Bake for 15 minutes; then carefully remove the foil and bake 5 minutes longer, or until the pastry is pale gold. Remove from the oven, leaving the oven on. Keep the springform pan on the jelly roll pan.

RHUBARB FILLING: In a saucepan, combine the rhubarb with ½ cup/ 100 g sugar over medium heat. Cook, stirring, until the rhubarb is tender and turns reddish, about 7 minutes. Set aside in a strainer to drain off excess liquid.

In a nonaluminum mixing bowl, whisk together the eggs, remaining ¼ cup plus 1 tablespoon/60 g sugar, cream, and vanilla. Whisk in the melted butter.

Spoon the rhubarb into the pastry shell. Place the tart pan still on the jelly roll pan or baking sheet on the center oven rack and carefully pour in the custard mixture.

Bake until the custard has set, 30 to 35 minutes. Cool the tart on a wire rack; then carefully remove the sides of the pan. Cover the tart with plastic wrap and refrigerate for at least 1 hour. Remove from the refrigerator about 10 minutes before serving. Just before serving, sprinkle the top of the outside edge with confectioners' sugar.

MAKES ONE 8- OR 9-INCH/20- OR 23-CM TART, SERVING ABOUT 8

❋

Fraisier

This traditional strawberry-and-cream cake is an elegant and colorful dessert all year round but it is especially succulent in late spring and summer, when local strawberries are in season.

The cream here is a combination of butter cream made with an Italian meringue (egg whites stabilized with sugar syrup), combined with a small proportion of pastry cream. For the home kitchen, chef Claude Moreau has suggested a simpler garnish for the top of the cake than the mirror-like glaze he applies in his shop.

BISCUIT GENOISE

5 LARGE EGGS

½ CUP PLUS 2 TABLESPOONS/ 110 G SUGAR

¾ CUP PLUS 2 TABLESPOONS/115 G ALL-PURPOSE FLOUR, SIFTED

¼ CUP (ROUNDED)/35 G GROUND ALMONDS

....

CRÈME PÂTISSIÈRE (PASTRY CREAM)

1 CUP/250 ML MILK

½ VANILLA BEAN, SPLIT LENGTHWISE, OR 1 TEASPOON VANILLA EXTRACT

3 LARGE EGG YOLKS

¼ CUP/50 G SUGAR

2 TABLESPOONS CORNSTARCH

....

CRÈME AU BEURRE (BUTTER CREAM)

¾ CUP/150 G SUGAR

½ CUP/125 ML WATER

3 LARGE EGG WHITES

1¼ CUPS (2½ STICKS) PLUS 2 TABLESPOONS/330 G UNSALTED BUTTER, CUT IN PIECES, SOFTENED

....

KIRSCH SOAKING SYRUP

⅓ CUP/60 G SUGAR

⅓ CUP/70 ML COLD WATER

1½ TABLESPOONS KIRSCH OR BRANDY

....

ASSEMBLY

1 TEASPOON VANILLA EXTRACT

3 PINTS RIPE STRAWBERRIES, HULLED

BISCUIT GENOISE: Preheat the oven to 375°F./190°C. Line a 10½ x 15½- inch/26 x 39-cm jelly roll pan with parchment or wax paper. Lightly butter the sides of the pan and the paper and set the pan aside.

Choose a saucepan in which a metal mixing bowl can be placed, with space between the bottom of the bowl and the bottom of the pan. Fill the saucepan about halfway with water—the water shouldn't touch the bottom of the bowl. Bring the water to a simmer. Place the eggs and sugar in the mixing bowl and place over the water. Whisk (or beat with a portable electric mixer) until the sugar has dissolved and the mixture is somewhat fluffy and just lukewarm, about 3 minutes.

Remove the bowl from the pan. Continue to whisk or blend the mixture at medium speed until the mixture is cool, pale, and about triple its original volume, about 8 minutes.

Sift the flour and almonds onto a sheet of wax paper. Add the flour mixture gradually to the egg mixture, folding it in very gently with a large rubber spatula. Gently scrape the batter into the prepared pan, spreading it gently and evenly with a rubber spatula. Bake until the cake is lightly golden and springs back lightly when pressed, 15 to 18 minutes. Cool the cake in the pan on a wire rack. Cover with plastic wrap until needed.

CRÈME PÂTISSIÈRE (PASTRY CREAM): Combine the milk and vanilla bean, if used, in a heavy saucepan and bring to a boil over medium heat. In a nonaluminum mixing bowl, whisk the egg yolks and sugar; add the cornstarch and whisk until well blended. Gradually pour the hot milk into the bowl and whisk to blend. Return the mixture to the saucepan and bring to a boil over medium heat. Boil, whisking vigorously, for 2 minutes. Strain the cream into a mixing bowl; if you are using vanilla extract, add it now. Place a sheet of plastic wrap directly onto the surface of the custard. Cool, then chill.

SLICES OF SUCCULENT STRAWBERRIES ADORN STOHRER'S ELEGANT VERSION
OF THE FRAISIER, A CLASSIC FRENCH STRAWBERRIES-AND-CREAM CAKE.

CRÈME AU BEURRE (BUTTER CREAM):
Bring the sugar and water to a boil in a small heavy saucepan over medium heat, stirring to dissolve the sugar. Let the mixture boil for 4 minutes, until it forms a soft ball (234–240°F./ 115°C). Meanwhile, beat the egg whites with an electric mixer until nearly stiff. As soon as the syrup is ready, with the mixer running, pour the syrup onto the beaters in a very thin, steady stream, until all the syrup is incorporated. Continue to beat until the mixture is fluffy and cooled to room temperature. Add the butter, one or two pieces at a time, until the mixture is well blended and fluffy. If the butter cream is not to be used immediately, refrigerate, covered. Remove from the refrigerator about ½ hour before using to soften and beat briefly to refluff.

KIRSCH SOAKING SYRUP: Combine the sugar and water in a saucepan over medium heat, stirring until the sugar has dissolved, about 4 minutes. Add the kirsch and remove from the

heat. Cool to room temperature.

ASSEMBLY: Combine the butter cream with 1 cup/250 ml of the pastry cream and 1 teaspoon vanilla extract, folding them together with a rubber spatula until smooth.

With a serrated knife, cut the edges from the cake. Cut the cake into two 6 x 8-inch/15 x 20-cm rectangles (reserve the remaining cake for another use). Place one rectangle of cake on a serving platter or a sheet of cardboard cut to fit. With a pastry brush, generously moisten the cake layer with some of the syrup. With a spatula, spread a ¼-inch/½-cm layer of the cream filling over the cake.

Cut the tops off several strawberries at their thickest point. Arrange these berries around the outside edges of the moistened iced cake, cut sides flush with the cake's edge, facing out. Set aside a few small strawberries for garnish. Arrange the remaining berries on their sides, covering the cake layer. Set a little of the cream filling aside. Place the remain-

ing cream in a pastry bag without a metal tip (or a plastic bag with a corner cut out) and cover the strawberries completely with the cream filling, without disturbing their position.

Place the second cake layer on top, pressing it gently. With a brush, soak the cake with the syrup. If necessary, smooth the edges of the cream with a spatula.

TOPPING: Spread the reserved cream over the top layer of cake, making a very smooth layer about ¼ inch/½ cm thick. If you like, hold a doily over the cake, sprinkle it with cocoa powder, then remove the doily, forming a lacy pattern. Chill until serving time. Place a few strawberries on top for garnish.

MAKES 6 SERVINGS

❀

Pâté aux Trois Viandes en Croûte

....

[THREE-MEAT PÂTÉ IN A CRUST]

....

PÂTE À PÂTÉ

½ CUP/125 ML WATER

1½ TEASPOONS WHITE WINE OR CIDER VINEGAR

1 TEASPOON SALT

2¾ CUPS/350 G ALL-PURPOSE FLOUR

¾ CUP (1½ STICKS)/180 G COLD UNSALTED BUTTER, CUT INTO PIECES

2 TABLESPOONS SUGAR

....

PÂTÉ MIXTURE

1 POUND/500 G CUBED BONELESS PORK SHOULDER WITH SOME FAT, WELL CHILLED

8 OUNCES/250 G CUBED BONE-LESS VEAL SHOULDER WITH SOME FAT, WELL CHILLED

4 OUNCES/225 G CUBED BONELESS RABBIT OR DARK MEAT OF CHICKEN, WELL CHILLED

1 SMALL ONION, CHOPPED

2 LARGE EGGS

2½ TABLESPOONS COGNAC

2 TEASPOONS SALT

½ TEASPOON FRESHLY GROUND BLACK PEPPER

¼ TEASPOON NUTMEG

¼ TEASPOON CLOVES

¼ TEASPOON GINGER

2 TABLESPOONS CORNSTARCH

....

ASSEMBLY

1 LARGE EGG, BEATEN,
FOR GLAZE

PÂTE À PÂTÉ: In a cup, stir together the water, vinegar, and salt. Place the flour, butter, and sugar in the bowl of an electric mixer or food processor. Mix until the ingredients are crumbly. Add the liquid mixture and mix just until combined. Be careful not to overmix. Gather the dough together, flatten it into a disk shape, and dust lightly with flour. Wrap in plastic and chill for at least 1 hour.

PÂTÉ MIXTURE: In a food processor, grind the cold meats until ground but not pasty. (A butcher can grind the meats for you.) Add the onion, eggs, Cognac, salt, pepper, nutmeg, cloves, ginger, and cornstarch. Pulse until well blended. To test the flavor, remove a rounded tablespoon of the mixture and form into a 1-inch/2½-cm patty. Cook the patty in a small skillet over medium heat until cooked through; taste and correct all seasonings. Cover the meat mixture and place in the refrigerator.

Cut off about one-quarter of the pastry and set aside. On a lightly floured surface, roll out the larger piece of pastry to an 8 x 14-inch/20 x 35-cm rectangle about ⅛ inch/⅓ cm thick. Roll the edges a little thinner than the rest of the pastry. Cut out a piece from each corner; reserve for another use. Carefully transfer the pastry to a nonstick or lightly buttered jelly roll pan dusted with a little flour.

Lay the meat mixture in the center of the pastry. With fingertips moistened in cold water, smooth the edges of the meat, mounding it neatly into a brick shape about 9 inches/23 cm long and 3 inches/8 cm wide. Brush the edges of the pastry with cold water. Now fold one long side of the pastry, then the other, up and over the meat to cover it compactly, overlapping the seams and pressing the pastry gently to seal. Brush the trian-

gular ends of the pastry lightly with cold water. Fold the ends up and over, as if wrapping a present, pressing them gently to adhere.

Roll the remaining piece of pastry to a rectangle about ⅛ inch/⅓ cm thick. Trim the edges neatly so that the rectangle fits the top of the pâté, approximately 9 x 3 inches/23 x 8 cm. Brush the top of the package with water, then gently lay the rectangle of pastry in place. Brush the top and sides of the pastry lightly with an egg wash. With the blunt side of a paring knife blade, trace a design in the pastry rectangle. Brush again with the egg wash. Cut several small slits along the length of the pâté to vent steam. Chill,

uncovered, for at least ½ hour.

Preheat the oven to 425°F./220°C. Paint the dough again with the egg glaze. Bake for 20 minutes, or until the pastry begins to brown lightly.

Lower the heat to 325°F./160°C. and continue to bake until the pastry is golden and a skewer inserted into the center of the meat comes out hot, at least 1 hour longer. The pâté is done when an instant-reading meat thermometer inserted into the center of the meat reads 165°F./80°C.

Cool the pâté on the pan on a wire rack to room temperature. Wrap in plastic and refrigerate overnight; then cut into slices and serve with cornichons.

SERVES 8 TO 10

....

THE PÂTÉ AUX TROIS VIANDES EN CROÛTE, A THREE-MEAT PÂTÉ
IN A FLAKY PASTRY CRUST, MAKES A PERFECT SIMPLE LUNCH WITH
A GLASS OF WINE, OR A TASTY STARTER FOR DINNER.

A SERENE ATMOSPHERE OF TEMPS PERDU PERVADES THE WOOD-PANELED DECOR OF LADURÉE.

Carrés aux Framboises

....

Financiers · Bostok

....

Le Royale

....

Le Royale au Café

....

Cake aux Fruits

Ladurée is an enchanting time capsule of nineteenth-century Paris, replete with romantic murals of cherubs cavorting on rose-hued clouds; tiny round and rectangular tables with beveled, black marble tops; panelled walls lushly adorned with gilded molding; and waitresses in prim, white-ruffled aprons.

A great part of this elegant tearoom's appeal, in addition to its finely crafted cakes, tarts, croissants, and tea sandwiches, is its timelessness and grace. An oasis from the blare and stress of contemporary urban life, Ladurée, opened in 1863, coddles and soothes. The clientele that crowds the little tables at lunchtime and later for tea is as immutable as the setting: chic ladies in chignons and perfectly tailored suits taking a break from the rigors of shopping on the nearby Faubourg-St.-Honoré; well-heeled older couples in for a day in the city; one or two somberly clad, lonely-looking women in their fifties— retired governesses, perhaps—extending three tea sandwiches into a two-hour lunch; and always a couple of tables of soignée mother-and-daughter duos.

Jean-Marie Desfontaines, the longtime owner and *chef-pâtissier*, is the second generation of his family at the helm of Ladurée, succeeding his father who acquired this venerable operation in 1943. The Desfontaines have perpetuated a tradition of handsomely presented *pâtisseries* in the *grand classique* mode. "Perhaps we've survived for so many years because we are more *exigeant*, more *raffiné*—more exacting in the preparation of our products, more refined in our decor and service—than many other places," says Chef Desfontaines, a demanding and vigilant *patron*. "And we have a very faithful clientele that returns week after week, year after year, and generation after generation." The customers come for some of the most beloved items in the repertory of French *pâtisserie*: flaky, burnished croissants; *financiers*, delicious dense and chewy almond cakes; celestial *macarons*, in a variety of hues and flavors; the *bostok*, an almond-topped, kirsch-bathed slice of recycled brioche; the *carré aux framboises*, a sugar-coated pastry "sandwich" filled with raspberry jam; and the *cake aux fruits*, a light, buttery pound cake laced with kirsch and studded with candied fruits. One specialty exclusive to the house is the popular *Royale,* a luscious, cream-filled cake in chocolate or coffee variations, named for the posh rue Royale, where Ladurée reigns at number 16, just up the street

LADURÉE'S GLEAMING GLASS CASES OFFER A VARIETY OF TEA SANDWICHES AS WELL AS A BOUNTY OF CLASSIC PÂTISSERIE.

. . . .

JEAN-MARIE DESFONTAINES HAS SUCCEEDED HIS FATHER AS THE EXACTING CHEF-OWNER OF LADURÉE.

from Maxim's and the Place de la Concorde.

Ladurée has had unusual staying power, remarkable even in this city with more respect for its patrimony than most others. (The components of the name, *La durée*, actually mean "endurance" or "continuance.") More striking even than its longevity is the fact that Ladurée has always been fashionable, thanks in large part to its position on a street that has long been synonymous with elegance and wealth. One hundred and thirty years of being "in"; few other establishments in this city can make such a claim. Flourishing in the days of Proust, Sarah Bernhardt, and Colette, Ladurée continues on as a gracious haven of *temps perdu* as the year 2000 approaches.

❋

Carrés aux Framboises

. . . .

[RASPBERRY SQUARES]

. . . .

PÂTE SABLÉE
3 CUPS/375 G ALL-PURPOSE FLOUR
1 CUP/200 G SUGAR
½ CUP/45 G SLICED BLANCHED ALMONDS
1 LARGE EGG, BEATEN

2½ STICKS/310 G UNSALTED BUTTER, CUT INTO PIECES, SOFTENED

. . . .

ASSEMBLY
1 LARGE EGG, BEATEN
¾ TO 1 CUP/175 TO 250 ML THICK RASPBERRY JAM, OR MORE AS NEEDED
SUGAR, PREFERABLY COARSE-CRYSTAL, FOR GARNISH

PÂTE SABLÉE: Place the flour, sugar, and almonds in the bowl of a food processor. Process until finely ground. Add the egg and butter and pulse until the dough begins to come together. Transfer the dough to a sheet of plastic wrap and gather dough together into a ball. Wrap well, and chill for at least ½ hour.

ASSEMBLY: Butter a 10½ x 15½-inch/26 x 39-cm jelly roll pan and set aside. Divide the dough in half. Roll one-half of the dough on a lightly floured surface to a thickness of ⅛ inch/⅓ cm. Fit it without stretching into the bottom of the pan; trim the edges neatly. Brush a 1-inch/2½-cm border around all the edges of the pastry with the beaten egg. Spread a ¼-inch-½-cm-thick layer of preserves over the bottom of the pastry, leaving the egg-washed border uncovered.

PERFECT WITH A CUP OF TEA ARE THE CRUMBLY AND DELICIOUS CARRÉS AUX FRAMBOISES, SUGAR-COATED PASTRIES FILLED WITH THICK RASPBERRY JAM.

. . . .

Preheat the oven to 350°F./175°C. Roll the remaining pastry ⅛ inch/⅓ cm thick to just fit inside the pan; gently lay it on top of the preserves, sandwiching the jam inside. Trim the edges to be flush with the sides of the pan; press the edges with your fingertips to seal the pastry. Brush the surface lightly with the beaten egg and sprinkle with the sugar. With a fork, prick holes all over the surface of the pastry.

Bake until the pastry is golden, 30 to 45 minutes. Cool on a wire rack in the pan; then trim off the sealed edges so that the jam shows, and cut the pastry into 3-inch/8-cm squares.

MAKES FIFTEEN 3-INCH/7-CM SQUARES

❋

Financiers

. . . .

[SMALL ALMOND CAKES]

. . . .

5 TABLESPOONS/75 G UNSALTED BUTTER, CUT INTO PIECES
5 TABLESPOONS SLICED OR SLIVERED BLANCHED ALMONDS
⅓ CUP/35 G CONFECTIONERS' SUGAR, LIGHTLY PACKED
¼ CUP PLUS 1 TABLESPOON/ 35 G ALL-PURPOSE FLOUR
3 LARGE EGG WHITES
½ TEASPOON VANILLA EXTRACT

Melt the butter in a small saucepan over moderate heat until lightly golden, about 3 to 4 minutes. Watch carefully to avoid burning. Pour the butter into a medium bowl, leaving behind any sediment in the pan.

Grind the almonds, sugar, and flour in a food processor until powdery. Add the egg whites and vanilla and mix briefly until smooth. Add the browned butter, mixing until blended. Cover with plastic wrap and refrigerate the batter overnight.

Preheat the oven to 350°F./175°C. Stir the mixture briefly to deflate it. Generously butter 10 *financier* molds (small trapezoid shapes), or use 1½ dozen small (1¾-inch/4-cm) muffin tins. Spoon the batter into the molds, dividing it evenly. Bake until golden, about 13 to 15 minutes for small muffin shapes, 15 to 20 minutes for larger *financiers*. Cool in the pan on a wire rack for about 5 minutes; then unmold and cool completely. Store airtight.

Note: In France, when *financiers* are baked in round molds, one blanched almond slice is usually placed on top. You can also bake the mixture in a buttered 8-inch/20-cm square pan, then cut the cake into rectangles.

MAKES 10 FINANCIERS (OR 16 TO 18 SMALL ROUNDS)

Bostok

. . . .

At Ladurée, this is made with brioche mousseline, a rich brioche baked in a tall cylindrical shape. You can use a charlotte mold or clean coffee can to bake the brioche, using Dalloyau's recipe on page 48, or use brioche slices from a loaf, such as Ganachaud's *Pain Brioché,* page 96.

8 SLICES BRIOCHE, ABOUT ¾ INCH/2 CM THICK

SYRUP

1 CUP/250 ML COLD WATER
⅔ CUP/160 G SUGAR
3 TABLESPOONS RUM, OR TO TASTE

. . . .

ALMOND CREAM

2 CUPS/175 G SLICED ALMONDS
2/3 CUP/160 G SUGAR
2 LARGE EGGS

GARNISH

½ CUP (SCANT)/20 G SLICED BLANCHED ALMONDS
CONFECTIONERS' SUGAR, FOR SPRINKLING

. . . .

FINANCIERS, LITTLE GOLDEN ALMOND CAKES, ARE A DELIGHTFUL AFTERNOON TREAT WITH A CUP OF COFFEE.

MANY HABITUÉS MAKE A LIGHT LUNCH OUT OF LADURÉE'S DAILY VARIETY OF TEA SANDWICHES.

A TEA-TIME TREAT CHEZ LADURÉE
IS CHEF DESFONTAINES'S BOSTOK, A
SLICE OF TOASTED BRIOCHE DRESSED
UP WITH KIRSCH AND ALMONDS.

....

Place the brioche slices on a wire rack over a jelly roll pan.

SYRUP: Heat the water and sugar over medium heat, stirring until the sugar has dissolved, about 4 minutes. Remove from the heat and stir in the rum. Brush the syrup generously over the top surfaces of the brioche.

ALMOND CREAM: Place the almonds and sugar in a food processor and grind until powdery. Add the eggs and process until the mixture forms a thick paste.

Preheat the oven to 400°F./200°C., with the rack in the upper third of the oven. Place the brioche slices on a baking sheet (do not use a dark metal pan) lined with parchment paper or well greased. With a thin spatula or butter knife, spread a layer of Almond Cream on the brioche, using about 2 tablespoons for each slice. Sprinkle each slice with a light coating of sliced almonds.

Bake until golden, about 14 minutes. Cool on a wire rack; then sprinkle very lightly with confectioners'

sugar and serve lukewarm or at room temperature.

MAKES 8 PIECES

❀

Le Royale

....

This luscious cake, a classic Ladurée recipe, can be made in either chocolate or coffee versions. This version is somewhat simplified from Jean-Marie Desfontaine's original, which is glazed *on top* of the chocolate *ganache* or coffee butter cream, with either a layer of chocolate fondant or a simple chocolate or coffee glaze.

CHOCOLATE CAKE

2 TABLESPOONS PLUS 1 TEA-
SPOON/35 G UNSALTED BUTTER,
CUT INTO PIECES

1 1/4 OUNCES/35 G SEMISWEET
CHOCOLATE, CHOPPED

7/8 CUP/80 G GROUND
BLANCHED ALMONDS

1/4 CUP PLUS 1 TABLESPOON/
55 G SUGAR

2 LARGE EGGS

2 LARGE EGG YOLKS

1/4 CUP PLUS 2 TEASPOONS/
35 G SIFTED FLOUR

....

GANACHE FILLING

1 CUP/250 ML CRÈME FRAÎCHE
OR HEAVY CREAM

8 OUNCES/240 G SEMISWEET
CHOCOLATE, CHOPPED

1/2 CUP/65 G CHOPPED TOASTED
ALMONDS, FOR GARNISH

CHOCOLATE CAKE: Preheat the oven to 350°F./175°C. Cut a sheet of parchment or wax paper to fit the bottom of an 8 x 4-inch/20 x 10-cm loaf pan. Lay the paper in the pan and butter the paper and sides of the pan; set aside.

Place the butter and chocolate in a small heavy saucepan over low heat. Stir until melted and smooth, about 5 minutes; then remove from the heat and set aside. Meanwhile, place the ground almonds, sugar, eggs, and egg yolks in a metal mixing bowl. Place the bowl over a pan

of simmering water and whisk until the mixture is lukewarm, about 3 minutes. Remove the bowl from the pan of water and beat with the whisk attachment of an electric mixer at high speed until the mixture forms a thick ribbon when dropped from the whisk, about 5 minutes.

Gently fold the chocolate mixture into the egg mixture. Sprinkle the flour over and gently fold together just until blended. Pour into the prepared pan and bake for 25 to 30 minutes, or until the center is set when pressed gently with a fingertip. Cool the cake in the pan on a wire rack for a few minutes. Then carefully invert the cake, peel off the paper, and cool the cake completely on the rack. If not filling right away, cover the cake with plastic wrap.

GANACHE FILLING: Bring the cream to a boil in a heavy saucepan over medium heat. Add the chopped chocolate and stir until melted and smooth, about 5 minutes. Transfer to a bowl and cool; then chill, stirring once or twice, just until cold but still liquid. Alternatively, set the bowl in a larger bowl of ice water and stir until it reaches the right consistency.

ASSEMBLY: With a long serrated knife, split the cake in 3 horizontal layers.

When the *ganache* mixture is cold, beat it with a whisk or an electric mixer with the whisk attachment. Beat until fluffy, about 4 minutes; do not overbeat, or the mixture will break down and become grainy. The whipped *ganache* should be used immediately.

Place the bottom layer on a long platter or a piece of cardboard cut slightly larger than the cake. With a spatula, spread about 1 cup/250 ml of the *ganache* on the layer. Gently place the second layer on top; spread with 1 cup/250 ml more of the filling. Gently replace the top layer. Spread the top and sides of the cake with the *ganache*. If you like, place

TWO TRADITIONAL FAVORITES CHEZ LADURÉE, LE ROYALE AU CHOCOLAT AND LE ROYALE AU CAFÉ,
ABOVE, ARE SOLD BOTH WHOLE AND BY THE SLICE FOR TEA.

. . . .

some of the *ganache* in a pastry bag (or a plastic sandwich bag with the corner cut out) and pipe decorations on top of the cake. Press chopped almonds along the outer edge. Refrigerate the cake.

Remove the cake from the refrigerator about ½ hour before serving and cut in slices.

MAKES 1 LOAF, ABOUT
8 SERVINGS

Le Royale au Café

. . . .

Chef Desfontaines makes a coffee *Royale* using the same chocolate cake and filling and topping it with coffee butter cream instead of the chocolate *ganache*.

1 RECIPE CHOCOLATE CAKE
(ABOVE)

. . . .

CRÈME BEURRE CAFÉ
(COFFEE BUTTER CREAM)

⅞ CUP/175 G SUGAR

½ CUP/125 ML WATER

6 LARGE EGG YOLKS

1¼ CUPS (2½ STICKS)/310 G
UNSALTED BUTTER, CUT INTO
PIECES, SOFTENED

1½ TABLESPOONS INSTANT COF-
FEE, PREFERABLY ESPRESSO OR
OTHER DARK ROAST

1 TABLESPOON HOT WATER

Prepare the cake as above. When cool, slice into 3 horizontal layers.
CRÈME BEURRE CAFÉ (COFFEE BUTTER CREAM): Bring the sugar and water to a boil in a small heavy saucepan over medium-low heat, stirring to dissolve the sugar, about 4

minutes. Let the mixture boil for 3 or 4 minutes, until it forms a soft ball (234–240°F./115°C.).

Meanwhile, beat the egg yolks with an electric mixer until fluffy. As soon as the syrup is ready, with the machine running, pour the syrup onto the beaters in a very thin, steady stream until all the syrup is incorporated. Continue to beat until the mixture is fluffy and cooled to room temperature.

Add the butter, 1 or 2 pieces at a time, beating until the mixture is well blended and fluffy. In a small cup, dissolve the instant coffee in the hot water; add to the butter cream and beat until well blended.

Assemble as for the chocolate *Royale*.

MAKES 1 LOAF, ABOUT
8 SERVINGS

MAX POILÂNE'S BOUCHONS, DENSE CHOCOLATE CUPCAKES IN THE FORM OF A
CHAMPAGNE CORK, ARE RICHLY STUDDED WITH CHOCOLATE CHIPS.

. . . .

somewhat moist. Cool the pan briefly on a wire rack; then gently unmold and cool the cakes completely.

MAKES 12 CAKES

❋

Pains de Méteil

. . . .

[RYE-WHOLE WHEAT ROLLS]

. . . .

This rustic bread was popular with the *citoyens* of the French Revolution, when precious white flour had to be used sparingly. Max Poilâne was asked to revive the recipe as part of France's bicentennial celebration in 1989.

4 TEASPOONS (ABOUT 1⅓ PACKAGES) DRY YEAST

2¼ CUPS/560 ML LUKEWARM WATER, OR MORE AS NEEDED

1 TABLESPOON PLUS 1 TEASPOON SALT

2¼ CUPS/280 G STONE-GROUND RYE FLOUR

2½ CUPS/310 G STONE-GROUND WHOLE WHEAT FLOUR

2½ CUPS/310 G UNBLEACHED WHITE FLOUR

Sprinkle the yeast on ½ cup/125 ml of the water; let stand for 10 minutes. Add the salt. Place the flours in a large mixing bowl (this dough is too stiff to be made in an electric mixer). Make a well in the center, and add the yeast mixture and remaining water. Knead briefly in the bowl, adding a little more water, if necessary, to bring the dough to a soft and silky but not sticky consistency (the dough will feel fairly heavy at this step). Turn the dough out onto a lightly floured surface and knead for 15 minutes.

Put the dough into a lightly oiled bowl, cover with a towel or plastic wrap, and let rise in a warm place until the dough has doubled in volume, 45 minutes to 1 hour. Punch the dough down, knead it for a moment in the bowl, then form it into a ball. Cover the bowl and let rise 45 minutes to 1 hour longer, or refrigerate overnight.

1⅓ CUPS/190 G ALL-PURPOSE FLOUR

⅔ CUP/120 G SEMISWEET CHOCOLATE CHIPS

Preheat the oven to 375°F./190°C. Butter twelve 2-inch/5-cm timbale molds or a muffin tin with twelve 2¾-inch/7-cm cups. In a large mixing bowl, whisk the eggs and sugar together until blended. Add the butter and cocoa and whisk until well blended and smooth. Add the flour and whisk until nearly blended. Stir in the chocolate chips just until the mixture is blended.

Spoon the batter into the molds or cups, filling them about three-quarters full. Bake 15 to 18 minutes (timing can vary based on the depth of the molds), or until the cakes have browned and set and a toothpick inserted in the center comes out

Petit Pain.
2ʄ10

DESSINS D'HENRI ISELIN

PAIN DE FROMENT
PAIN DE SEIGLE
PAIN DE SEIGLE AUX RAISINS
PAIN AUX NOIX

A HILLOCK OF PETITS PAINS, WHITE DINNER ROLLS, IS FREQUENTLY REPLENISHED THROUGHOUT THE DAY.

SINFULLY RICH IS AN UNDERSTATEMENT WHEN IT COMES TO ROBERT LINXE'S UNIQUE CHOCOLATE CAKE, LE PLEYEL.

ROBERT LINXE'S LACY, CHOCOLATE-BOTTOMED FLORENTINS ARE CHEWY WITH CANDIED FRUIT AND ALMONDS.

Florentins

....

These delectable chocolate-bottomed cookies, with a play of textures and flavors in every bite, are a hit every time I serve them. Robert Linxe's personal variation on a classic cookie owes its appeal to the mixture of dried and candied fruits used with the almonds, the combination accented by his signature chocolate. Choose the best-quality orange rind and candied cherries you can find.

2 3/4 CUPS/200 G SLICED
BLANCHED ALMONDS

1/2 CUP/125 ML HEAVY CREAM

7 TABLESPOONS/100 G UNSALTED
BUTTER, CUT INTO PIECES

1/4 CUP PLUS 3 TABLESPOONS/
100 G SUGAR

2 TABLESPOONS PLUS
1 TEASPOON HONEY

1/3 CUP (LIGHTLY PACKED)/
50 G CANDIED CHERRIES,
CHOPPED FINE

1/4 CUP/50 G CANDIED ORANGE
RIND, CHOPPED FINE

1/3 CUP/50 G ALL-PURPOSE FLOUR

8 OUNCES/250 G SEMISWEET
OR BITTERSWEET CHOCOLATE,
CHOPPED

Preheat the oven to 375°F./190°C. Spread the almonds on a baking sheet and toast them, stirring once or twice, until lightly golden, about 8 minutes. Set aside to cool.

In a saucepan, heat the cream, butter, sugar, and honey over medium heat, stirring, until the mixture is melted and comes to a boil. Boil without stirring for about 3 minutes, until the mixture comes to a temperature of about 230°F. (120°C.), or until it forms a soft ball when a small amount is dropped into a cup of ice water. Remove from the heat.

Stir in the toasted almonds, chopped cherries, and orange rind, then stir in the flour until blended. Pour the mixture into a buttered 9-inch/23-cm square baking pan and set aside to cool. Cover with plastic wrap and let stand at room temperature overnight, or for at least 1 hour.

Preheat the oven to 425°F./220°C. Scoop up tablespoonfuls of the mixture and place on a buttered baking sheet, spacing them well apart, or in buttered tartlet pans, just covering the bottoms. With the back of a fork dipped in cold water, pat the mixture as thin as possible. Bake until the cookies are golden, 5 to 6 minutes. Watch carefully to prevent burning. If you are baking the florentines on a baking sheet, gently push in the edges with a fork as soon as they are done, to form even rounds. Cool for about 4 minutes.

When the florentines are still warm, gently coax them from the pan with a spatula and transfer to a wire rack covered with parchment paper to cool.

Melt the chocolate over hot water just until smooth but not too hot. With a spatula, spread the smooth bottom surface of each florentine evenly with chocolate and place on the parchment paper, chocolate-side up. If you like, with a pastry comb or fork, trace a pattern of wavy lines in the chocolate before it becomes firm. Stored airtight, these cookies will keep for almost 2 weeks.

MAKES ABOUT 2 DOZEN COOKIES

❋

Délice

....

This is Robert Linxe's adaptation for home cooks of his famous Délice, a chocolate-cream-and-chocolate-macaroon cake. In his shop this complex confection is made with an ultra-thin white-macaroon base layer, which he deletes from the recipe below.

MACAROON CAKE
1 1/8 CUPS/100 G SLICED
BLANCHED ALMONDS

3/4 CUP/100 G CONFECTIONERS'
SUGAR

1/3 CUP/30 G UNSWEETENED
COCOA POWDER

6 LARGE EGG WHITES,
AT ROOM TEMPERATURE

2 TABLESPOONS GRANULATED
SUGAR

PINCH OF SALT

....

GANACHE
1/2 CUP/125 ML HEAVY CREAM

1/2 CUP/125 ML COLD WATER

1 POUND/500 G BITTERSWEET
OR SEMISWEET CHOCOLATE,
CUT INTO PIECES

7 TABLESPOONS/100 G UNSALTED
BUTTER, SOFTENED

MACAROON CAKE: Preheat the oven to 375°F./190°C. Line a 10 1/2 x 15 1/2-inch/26 x 39-cm jelly roll pan with parchment or wax paper. Spray the sides of the pan and the paper with nonstick cooking spray or butter lightly. Set the pan aside.

In a food processor, grind the almonds with the confectioners' sugar until powdery. Sift this mixture into a bowl, then add the cocoa and stir to combine.

Beat the egg whites until they begin to become frothy; then add the granulated sugar and salt. Continue to beat until the whites form stiff peaks. With a large rubber spatula, very gently fold the almond-cocoa mixture thoroughly into the beaten egg whites. Gently scrape the batter into the prepared pan, spreading it evenly.

Bake until the cake springs back lightly when pressed in the center, about 12 minutes. Cool the cake in the pan on a wire rack. Cover the cake with plastic wrap and refrigerate overnight. (The cake can also be prepared in advance, wrapped tightly, and frozen.)

GANACHE: Bring the cream and water to a boil in a saucepan over medium heat. Stir in the chocolate and let stand for 1 minute, stirring once or twice. Continue stirring until the chocolate is melted and smooth. Remove 1/2 cup/120 g of this mixture and refrigerate; this will be used later to glaze the top. Cool the remaining *ganache* to lukewarm. Beat in the softened butter, a tablespoon or two at a time. Set aside to cool at room temperature, or to hasten the cooling, place the mixture in the refrigerator, stirring once or twice, until very cold but still liquid.

Remove the plastic wrap from the

cake. Run a knife blade around the edges and invert it onto a work surface. Gently peel off the paper. With a serrated knife, cut the edges off the cake all around. Cut the cake crosswise into 3 strips 9 inches/23 cm long and 3½ inches/9 cm wide; reserve the trimmings for another use.

With an electric mixer at medium-high speed, whip the *ganache*-butter mixture until fluffy, about 2 minutes, or whip with a wire whisk until fluffy. Do not overbeat, or the mixture will break down and become grainy.

Place 1 cake layer on a plate or a piece of cardboard cut to fit. With a spatula, spread a thick layer of the whipped *ganache* over the cake, using about 1½ cups of the *ganache*. Lay a second cake layer over the *ganache* and top with another thick layer of *ganache*. Lay the third cake layer on top, and gently spread a thinner layer of *ganache* over the top. Refrigerate the cake briefly to firm up the *ganache* slightly. Smooth the sides with a metal spatula, moving it horizontally to tidy up the icing without smearing the layers. Refrigerate the cake, loosely wrapped in plastic, for several hours or overnight; it should be very well chilled.

Warm the reserved unwhipped chilled *ganache* in a double boiler or in a metal bowl over simmering water, cutting and stirring the mixture until just pourable and barely tepid. With a spatula, spread the fluid *ganache* over the top of the cake. Work quickly so the tepid *ganache* doesn't melt the filling. With a fork or knife, trace a pattern of lines into the glaze. Refrigerate the cake, well wrapped, for at least 1 hour and up to overnight. Remove from the refrigerator 20 to 30 minutes before cutting in slices. The cake should be served at cool room temperature but not too cold.

SERVES ABOUT 8

. . . .

A SIDE VIEW OF LA MAISON DU CHOCOLAT'S DÉLICE CAKE REVEALS THE LUSCIOUS, MOUSSEY INTERIOR OF THIS INTENSELY FLAVORED CONFECTION.

PETITS MACARONS
PETITS PLEYELS
SABLES
35 Fr LES 100 GR

THE WINDOW DISPLAY AT LA MAISON DU CHOCOLAT IS A CHOCOHOLIC'S DREAM COME TRUE.

LERCH'S TARTE AU FROMAGE BLANC IS AT HOME AMID THE DECOR OF AUX COEURS D'ALSACE, A NEARBY SHOP.

Pain d'Épices · Kugelhopf

....

Tarte au Fromage-Blanc

Tarte à l'Oignon · Madeleines

....

Sablés à la Cannelle

....

Tarte aux Abricots

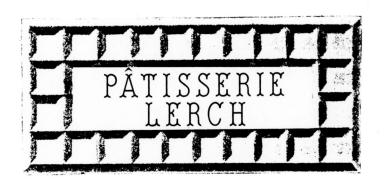

Behind the unassuming facade of his Left Bank *pâtisserie-boulangerie,* with its fraying awning faded a murky red, André Lerch produces dazzling masterworks of Alsatian pastry so fresh and vibrant they seem to emanate light. Fragrant, lemony *madeleines,* the tea cakes of Proustian fame; glistening fruit tarts—apricot, pear, apple, plum— savory onion and bacon tarts; airy, almond-studded *kugelhopfs*—Alsatian coffee cakes—and dense, aromatic spice breads are displayed on the cramped counter-space presided over by Madame Dénise, his wife. These are but a few of the regional delights this energetic and prolific pastry chef and baker produces over each long day.

Born in Strasbourg, where he began his pastry *apprentissage* at the age of fourteen, just after World War II, Monsieur Lerch has been creating his native *pâtisseries* in Paris for forty years. Among his clientele, largely a faithful coterie of neighbors that includes singer Georges Moustaki and Catherine Deneuve, as well as the polite young firemen from a nearby station, are some of the top bistros of the Latin Quarter and even the Tour d'Argent. A jovial, beaming presence, his trimmed white hair always slightly ruffled, Monsieur Lerch is a well-known figure in his Left Bank world. He makes his own deliveries in his little white truck, stopping for pleasantries and conversation seemingly at every corner. At Christmastime his earnest, open face can be seen even

ANDRÉ LERCH, STANDING BEFORE HIS SHOP ON THE RUE
CARDINAL-LEMOINE, HOLDS TWO CLASSIC KUGELHOPFS, WHICH
HE BAKES DAILY IN A VARIETY OF SIZES.

Pain d'Épices

. . . .

[SPICE BREAD]

. . . .

This wonderfully aromatic and light-ly honeyed bread is delicious with café au lait or a cup of full-bodied tea. Well-wrapped in foil, it can last up to a week.

³⁄₄ CUP/175 ML HONEY

¹⁄₂ CUP/100 G LIGHT BROWN
SUGAR

³⁄₄ CUP/175 ML WATER

2 CUPS/250 G ALL-PURPOSE
FLOUR, LIGHTLY SPOONED INTO
A MEASURING CUP (ABOUT
9 OUNCES)

1 LARGE EGG, BEATEN

1 LARGE EGG YOLK

1 ¹⁄₂ TEASPOONS BAKING POWDER

1 TEASPOON BAKING SODA

1 ¹⁄₂ TEASPOONS GROUND
ANISE SEEDS

1 ¹⁄₂ TEASPOONS ALLSPICE

1 ¹⁄₂ TEASPOONS CINNAMON

1 ¹⁄₂ TEASPOONS NUTMEG

1 ¹⁄₂ TEASPOONS GINGER

³⁄₄ TEASPOON GROUND CLOVES

Preheat the oven to 350°F./175°C. Butter a 9 x 5-inch/23 x 13-cm loaf pan, and set aside.

In a saucepan, bring the honey, brown sugar, and water to a boil. Boil gently over medium heat, stirring once or twice, uncovered, for 5 min-utes. Remove from the heat and gradually sift in 1 cup/125 g of the flour, whisking steadily. Set aside.

In a large mixing bowl, whisk the egg and yolk until frothy. Sift the remaining cup of flour with the bak-ing powder, baking soda, anise seeds, allspice, cinnamon, nutmeg, ginger, and cloves. Add the honey mixture to the eggs; then add the sifted ingredi-ents. Mix just until blended, then pour the mixture into the loaf pan. Bake until the bread is firm to the touch and has begun to pull away from the sides of the loaf pan, about 45 minutes. Cool in the pan on a wire rack.

SERVES 6 TO 8

on television discussing regional hol-iday specialties as crowds line up out-side his door for his famous *pain d'épices*, traditional Alsatian spice bread.

"To succeed in this *métier*, you have to love it," Monsieur Lerch says. "I live for my business. For me it's like our child. You can't begrudge the time it takes to do the work prop-erly, even if it sometimes comes before family." He arrives in his *lab-oratoire*, or pastry kitchen, at 4:45 A.M. to begin the quiche Lorraines, the *tartelettes*, and the *kugelhopfs*, aided by a staff of six. Madame Lerch opens the shop at seven. At nine Monsieur Lerch is on his way to Rungis, the sprawling wholesale pro-duce market outside of Paris, to choose the fruits for his daily tarts. ("Ordering the produce to be deliv-ered is never the same as going your-

self," he notes. "It's the quality of your ingredients that brings your customers back.") Then it's back to his shop where he prepares lunch for his personnel. The two- to four-o'-clock slot is reserved for his siesta. The kitchens close at four and the staff departs, but Monsieur Lerch often remains alone, working on spe-cial orders and decorating cakes.

From 6:30 to 8:00 in the evening is perhaps Monsieur Lerch's favorite slice of the day. In the hazy Paris dusk, he slides back behind the wheel of his little truck and makes his last deliveries to restaurants and clubs—the Tour d'Argent, Le Petit Navire, the Paradis-Latin—accept-ing the proffered *verres* as he goes. "To see if the Beaujolais is still good," he says with a wink. "This is my little end-of-the-day tour," he adds, "my *campagne electorale!*"

HEADY WITH SPICES AND HONEY, MONSIEUR LERCH'S PAIN D'EPICE, ALSATIAN SPICE BREAD,
IS DELICIOUS WITH A CUP OF SMOKY LAPSANG SOOCHANG TEA.

Kugelhopf

[ALSATIAN COFFEE CAKE]

1 CUP/140 G GOLDEN RAISINS

¼ CUP/60 ML KIRSCH OR BRANDY

2½ CUPS/625 ML LUKEWARM MILK

1 CUP (2 STICKS)/240 G
UNSALTED BUTTER, SOFTENED

5 TEASPOONS (2 PACKAGES)
DRY YEAST

5½ CUPS/685 G ALL-PURPOSE
FLOUR, OR MORE AS NEEDED

SOFTENED BUTTER FOR MOLDS

½ CUP/90 G WHOLE
BLANCHED ALMONDS

¾ CUP PLUS 2 TABLESPOONS/
200 G GRANULATED SUGAR

4 TEASPOONS SALT

2 LARGE EGGS

CONFECTIONERS' SUGAR,
FOR DUSTING

In a small bowl, soak the raisins in the kirsch; set aside while the dough is being prepared.

STARTER: In a saucepan, gently heat ¾ cup/175 ml of the milk with 4 tablespoons/60 g of the butter over low heat until lukewarm. Transfer to a mixing bowl and sprinkle on the yeast, then stir in 1 cup/125 g of the flour until almost completely incorporated. Cover the bowl loosely with plastic wrap and let rise in a draft-free place until the mixture almost doubles in volume, about 1 hour.

Generously butter two 2-quart/2-liter *kugelhopf* or Bundt pans. Press the almonds into the grooves at the bottom (crown) of each, so they stay in place.

In a large mixing bowl or an electric mixer with a dough hook attachment, combine the remaining lukewarm milk, butter, and flour with the granulated sugar, salt, and eggs. Mix thoroughly until blended. Add the starter and mix until blended. Knead by hand on a lightly floured

surface, or with an electric mixer at medium-high speed, for about 10 minutes, or until the dough is smooth and supple, feeling soft and very slightly sticky. As you knead, add a little more flour or milk if necessary to adjust the consistency.

Drain the raisins, reserving the liquid, and knead them into the dough by hand in the bowl until well distributed. Cover the bowl with plastic wrap and let the dough rise to 1½ times its volume, 1 to 1 ½ hours.

Preheat the oven to 375°F./190°C, with the rack about one-third of the way up from the bottom. Divide the dough in 2 equal pieces. Gather each one into a ball, make a 1-inch/2½-cm hole in the middle of the dough with your thumb, and fit the dough into the mold, arranging it evenly. The mold should be about three-quarters full. Cover loosely and let the dough rise for 5 to 10 minutes.

THE KUGELHOPF IS BEST BAKED IN A TRADITIONAL EARTHENWARE MOLD, SUCH AS THESE FROM AUX COEURS D'ALSACE.

Bake until the *kugelhopfs* are golden brown and sound hollow when tapped, about 45 minutes. Cover with a sheet of foil about halfway through the baking time if the surface of the *kugelhopfs* is beginning to brown too quickly. If you'd like a slightly crisper loaf, remove it from the pan and place the cake directly on the oven rack for the last 3 or 4 minutes of baking.

Cool in the pans for a few minutes on a wire rack; then unmold the *kugelhopfs* and cool thoroughly. Drizzle the leftover kirsch into the center of the cakes; then dust liberally with confectioners' sugar. Cover well with plastic wrap or put in a plastic bag to store. In Alsace, the *kugelhopf* is never served on the same day it is baked. It is made the night before, or even 2 days ahead, so it can "age" to the right light, dry texture. Dust again with confectioners' sugar just before serving.

MAKES TWO 8- TO 9-INCH KUGEL-HOPFS, EACH SERVING 6 TO 8

❋

Tarte au Fromage-Blanc ✓

....

[ALSATIAN CHEESE CAKE]

....

If French *fromage blanc* is unavailable, you can use Vermont *fromage blanc* (see mail-order sources, page 156). A combination of ricotta and cream cheese also results in a similar smooth, light curd texture, but is not as accurate a representation of André Lerch's singular cheese cake as is one made with *fromage blanc.*

PÂTE BRISÉE

1¼ CUPS/155 G ALL-PURPOSE FLOUR

2 TABLESPOONS SUGAR

¼ TEASPOON SALT

4 TABLESPOONS/60 G COLD UNSALTED BUTTER, CUT INTO PIECES

4 TABLESPOONS COLD MILK, OR AS NEEDED

....

FILLING

3 LARGE EGGS, SEPARATED

1 TABLESPOON ALL-PURPOSE FLOUR

3 TABLESPOONS CORNSTARCH

¼ TEASPOON VANILLA EXTRACT

GRATED ZEST OF 1 LEMON

2 POUNDS/1 KG FROMAGE BLANC (OR 1 POUND EACH RICOTTA CHEESE AND CREAM CHEESE, MIXED)

½ CUP/100 G SUGAR

PÂTE BRISÉE: In a food processor or medium bowl, mix the flour, sugar, salt, and butter together until crumbly. Add just enough milk for the dough to come together. Gather it into a ball; then knead briefly on a lightly floured surface, just until the dough is smooth. Wrap in plastic and chill for at least 1 hour.

On a lightly floured surface, roll the dough into a 12-inch/30-cm circle. Fit it, without stretching, into a generously buttered 9- or 10-inch/23- or 25-cm tart pan with a removable bottom, preferably one with smooth sides. Trim off the excess dough. Chill the pastry shell.

FILLING: Preheat the oven to 400°F./200°C. In a mixing bowl, beat the egg yolks; then add the flour, cornstarch, vanilla, and lemon zest and whisk just until smooth. Stir in the *fromage blanc,* or ricotta and cream cheeses, until smooth.

Beat the egg whites until they form soft peaks. Gradually add the sugar and continue beating until the whites form stiff peaks but are not dry. Gently fold the beaten whites into the cheese mixture. Pour into the pastry shell and place on the center oven rack. After about 15 minutes, carefully run a thin spatula between the crust and the edges of the mold to prevent sticking. Then, when the cheese filling begins to rise above the crust, after 15 or 20 minutes, gently make a thin cut around the edge of the filling just above the crust, holding a paring knife

horizontally; this will let air escape.

Continue to bake until the filling is set and the surface has browned lightly, about 40 minutes. If the surface of the tart becomes too brown before the filling has set, gently lay a sheet of aluminum foil over the surface and continue to bake.

Cool the tart on a wire rack; then carefully unmold the tart and transfer it to a platter.

SERVES 8 TO 10

❋

Tarte à l'Oignon

....

[ALSATIAN SAVORY ONION TART]

....

PÂTE BRISÉE

1 CUP/125 G ALL-PURPOSE FLOUR

¼ TEASPOON SALT

4 TABLESPOONS/60 G COLD UNSALTED BUTTER

3 TABLESPOONS COLD WATER, PLUS MORE AS NEEDED

....

FILLING

3½ OUNCES/105 G SLAB BACON, CUT INTO ½-INCH/1-CM CUBES

2 TABLESPOONS UNSALTED BUTTER

1 POUND/500 G ONIONS (ABOUT 4 MEDIUM), THINLY SLICED

2 TABLESPOONS ALL-PURPOSE FLOUR

2 LARGE EGGS

½ CUP/125 ML CRÈME FRAÎCHE OR HEAVY CREAM

½ TEASPOON SALT (OPTIONAL)

PÂTE BRISÉE: Combine the flour and the salt in a mixing bowl and form a well in the center. Add the butter and cut the mixture together with a pastry cutter, or pulse the mixture if using a food processor, until crumbly. Add the water and stir the dough vigorously, or pulse in a food processor, until the dough comes together. Add 1 to 2 more tablespoons of water if the dough is dry. The dough should be soft but not sticky. Form the dough into a ball, wrap it in plastic, and chill for ½ hour.

THE TARTE À L'OIGNON, SORT OF AN ALSATIAN "PIZZA," IS PERFECT
FOR A LIGHT SUPPER OR SLICED INTO HORS D'OEUVRES.

....

Roll the dough on a lightly floured surface to a thin 11-inch/28-cm circle and transfer it without stretching to a 9-inch/23-cm tart pan with a removable bottom, preferably black tin or steel. Trim the edges and place the tart pan on a baking sheet.

FILLING: Preheat the oven to 400°F./200°C. In a heavy-bottomed skillet, sauté the bacon cubes over medium heat, stirring, until lightly golden, about 8 minutes. Transfer the bacon to a paper towel–lined plate. Pour off all but 1 or 2 tablespoons of the bacon fat from the pan, then add the butter. Sauté the onions over medium heat, stirring occasionally, until they are tender and transparent, about 10 minutes; do not let them brown. Stir in the flour, then remove the pan from the heat and set aside.

In a mixing bowl, beat together the eggs, crème fraîche or cream, and the optional salt. Stir the bacon and the onion mixture into the egg mixture until combined. Pour the filling into the crust.

Bake the tart until the pastry and filling are lightly golden, 30 to 35 minutes. Cool for 5 minutes on a wire rack, then carefully remove the sides of the tart pan. Serve hot, cut into wedges.

SERVES 6

....

Note: This tart can also be made free-form on a baking sheet, pizza style. Roll out the dough to a 13-inch/33-cm circle and gently transfer to a baking sheet. Brush the edge of the dough with cold water and roll the edge in about 1 inch/2½ cm to form a border.

❋

Madeleines

....

2 LARGE EGGS

½ CUP/100 G SUGAR

5 TABLESPOONS/75 G UNSALTED BUTTER, MELTED AND COOLED SLIGHTLY

¾ CUP/100 G ALL-PURPOSE FLOUR

1 TEASPOON BAKING POWDER

GRATED ZEST OF ½ LEMON

¼ TEASPOON VANILLA EXTRACT

In a large mixing bowl or the bowl of an electric mixer, whisk or blend the eggs and sugar until frothy. Add the cooled melted butter, blending well. On low speed or with the whisk, add the flour, baking powder, lemon zest, and vanilla until blended. Cover the bowl with a towel and set aside to rest for 1 hour.

Preheat the oven to 375°F./190°C. Butter and flour the madeleine molds. Whisk the batter for a moment to remix, then spoon the batter lightly into the molds, filling them three-quarters full. Bake until the cakes are risen and golden, 10 or 11 minutes. If the madeleines start to brown before the crown has risen, open the oven door slightly and continue to bake until they have risen.

As soon as the madeleines are done, carefully remove them from the tins onto a wire rack. Serve immediately. The madeleines can also be cooled on a rack and stored for several days in an airtight container.

MAKES ABOUT 15 MADELEINES

❋

Sablés à la Cannelle

....

[CINNAMON SHORTBREAD COOKIES]

....

½ CUP PLUS 3 TABLESPOONS/ 50 G SLICED ALMONDS

1⅞ CUPS/235 G ALL-PURPOSE FLOUR

1 TEASPOON BAKING POWDER

7 TABLESPOONS/110 G SOFTENED UNSALTED BUTTER

½ CUP/100 G SUGAR

2 LARGE EGGS

2 TEASPOONS CINNAMON

GRATED ZEST OF 1 LEMON

1 EGG, BEATEN, FOR GLAZE

Grind the almonds with ½ cup/60 g of the flour in a food processor. Sift this mixture with the remaining flour and the baking powder into a mixing bowl or onto a work surface.

THE CLASSIC AND, TO MARCEL PROUST, INSPIRATIONAL MADELEINE IS DISTINGUISHED BY ITS UNIQUE SHELL SHAPE.

LERCH'S VIBRANT TARTE AUX ABRICOTS PICKS UP THE COLORS OF HAND-PAINTED ALSATIAN FURNITURE.

Make a well in the middle of the flour mixture and add the butter, sugar, 2 eggs, cinnamon, and lemon zest. If working with your hands, gradually work the flour into the remaining ingredients, rubbing them together between your fingers. If using an electric mixer, start at slow speed and mix until the ingredients are well combined, scraping the mixture down from the sides of the bowl once or twice. Divide the mixture in half. Place each half of the dough between 2 sheets of plastic wrap. Gently flatten each piece and chill for at least 1 hour.

Butter 2 baking sheets. Working with half of the dough at a time, roll the dough between the sheets of plastic wrap to a thickness of about ⅛ inch/⅓ cm. With cookie cutters, cut the dough in a variety of shapes and transfer to the baking sheet. Lightly brush the surfaces of the cookies with the beaten egg. Set aside for 10 minutes to allow the egg to dry.

Preheat the oven to 400°F./ 200°C., with a rack at the center level. Brush the cookies with another layer of egg. Bake the cookies until golden, 8 to 12 minutes. Monsieur Lerch cautions that you shouldn't remove the cookies from the oven too soon; because the cinnamon-tinted dough is dark, they can look like they are done before they actually are. Cool the pan on a wire rack for about 5 minutes; then transfer the cookies to the rack and cool completely. Store airtight.

MAKES ABOUT 4 DOZEN COOKIES

Tarte aux Abricots

....

[ANDRÉ LERCH'S SPECIAL APRICOT TART]

....

If fresh apricots are not in season, you can also make this beautiful tart with canned apricots, draining them well on a paper towel–lined plate.

The filling in this tart is Monsieur Lerch's own creation. It is a batter that rises to become a very thin "cake" layer, similar to a *quatre-quarts*, or pound cake. He uses it to absorb the juices of the fresh fruit and to help bind the fruit to the tart.

PÂTE BRISÉE AU SUCRE

1½ CUPS/210 G ALL-PURPOSE FLOUR

½ CUP/100 G SUGAR

⅛ TEASPOON BAKING POWDER

½ CUP (1 STICK)/50 G UNSALTED BUTTER, CUT INTO PIECES, CHILLED

1 LARGE EGG, BEATEN

....

FILLING

1 LARGE EGG

¼ CUP/30 G SUGAR

½ TEASPOON VANILLA EXTRACT

¼ CUP/50 G ALL-PURPOSE FLOUR

⅛ TEASPOON BAKING POWDER

4 TABLESPOONS (½ STICK)/ 50 G UNSALTED BUTTER, SOFTENED

....

FRUIT

25 TO 30 (ABOUT 3 POUNDS/ 1.5 KG) FRESH, BUT NOT TOO RIPE, APRICOTS, HALVED AND PITTED, OR AS NEEDED (OR USE 3½ TO 4 POUNDS/750 G TO 2 KG CANNED APRICOTS, WELL DRAINED)

2 TABLESPOONS GRANULATED SUGAR

CONFECTIONERS' SUGAR, FOR SPRINKLING

PÂTE BRISÉE AU SUCRE: Combine the flour, sugar, and baking powder in a mixing bowl and form a well in the center, or blend in a food processor. Add the butter and cut the mixture together until crumbly. Add the egg and stir the combined ingredients vigorously until the dough comes together, pulsing the mixture if using a food processor. Flatten the dough in a disk shape, wrap it in plastic, and chill for at least ½ hour.

Roll the pastry on a lightly floured sheet of wax paper or plastic wrap into a 13-inch/33-cm circle about ⅛ inch/⅓ cm thick, lightly dusting the pastry with flour as needed. Chill the pastry briefly to

make it easier to handle. Carefully invert the pastry, wax paper–side up, to a buttered 10- or 11-inch/25- or 28-cm false-bottomed tart pan, fitting it without stretching, and pressing the dough to fit the fluted sides of the pan. Carefully peel off the wax paper and trim the edges. You can also fit the pastry into a buttered 9-inch/23-cm springform pan, forming even sides about 1½ inches/4 cm high. Refrigerate the pastry shell for at least ½ hour.

FILLING: Preheat the oven to 400°F./ 200°C., with racks in the lower third and upper third of the oven. In a mixing bowl, whisk together the egg, sugar, and vanilla. Sift the flour and baking powder into the egg mixture, stirring gently with a wooden spoon until just combined. Add the butter and mix just until the batter is smooth. With a spatula, spread this mixture over the bottom and sides of the crust.

FRUIT: If you are using canned apricots, arrange them on a paper towel–lined plate and pat the tops with a paper towel to remove excess moisture. Arrange the apricot halves over the filling, standing them up with the edges upward in concentric circles, overlapping slightly, to cover the filling completely.

Bake the tart on the lowest oven shelf for 25 minutes, or until the crust is golden brown. Carefully transfer the tart to the top shelf. Sprinkle the apricots with granulated sugar, taking care not to sugar the pastry, or it will become too brown. Bake the tart until the apricots are glazed with gold, about 15 minutes longer. About 5 minutes before the tart is done, prop the oven door slightly ajar with a wooden spoon, so that steam can escape and the pastry doesn't become soggy. Transfer the tart to a wire rack and cool completely.

Just before serving, sprinkle the crust and edges of the tart with confectioners' sugar. Serve at room temperature, cut in wedges.

SERVES 8 TO 10

Les Grands Classiques

LENÔTRE

GANACHAUD

MARCEL HAUPOIS

GASTON LENÔTRE'S SAVARIN AU CHANTILLY IS AN ELEGANT VARIATION ON THE BABA AU RHUM.

Paris-Brest

....

Savarin au Chantilly

....

Tarte aux Noix

In the history of twentieth-century *pâtisserie*, there is no one who casts a longer shadow than Gaston Lenôtre. This peripatetic, silver-haired septuagenarian is the emperor, the oracle, the capo di capi. Almost every neighborhood in Paris today has its Pâtisserie Lenôtre and the map of the world, from Tokyo to Riyad, is dotted with others. Monsieur Lenôtre's domain is vast. But more important than the scope of his business is what he has wrought in his métier—the changes he has made in the character and taste of his own *pâtisseries,* and by example and success, the influence he has had on contemporary French *pâtisserie.*

The Lenôtre enterprise is a far cry from the small, traditional Paris neighborhood bakeshop represented by many other *pâtisseries* and *boulangèries* in this book. But Lenôtre confections and comestibles are still made using classic artisanal techniques, albeit on a very grand scale. The work is done by hand as well as by machines replicating artisanal techniques, such as those that roll out large sheets of dough to a perfect, uniform depth. Everything sold in the fourteen Lenôtre boutiques in Paris and the Ile-de-France is produced at a central headquarters in the small and appropriately named Paris suburb of Plaisir.

The plant at Plaisir hums with virtually nonstop activity, supplying the many different neighborhood shops, most open seven days a week, twelve hours a day, with up to a thousand different products. Lenôtre also does a major catering business, producing feasts for a large variety of public and private celebrations, from banquets for heads of state, such as the Summit at Versailles several years back, and the annual luncheon at the exclusive Prix de Diane horse race in Chantilly, to lavish family birthday parties. "One of the great pleasures of my business," says Monsieur Lenôtre, "is that I can be part of many happy events in the lives of my customers—marriages, communions, baptisms. I love all these traditional events." He also loves traditional recipes, particularly from the provinces, from the classic apple *tarte Normande* from his native Normandy, to a Tarte aux Noix—a walnut tart—flavored with brown sugar and Grand Marnier, from the Périgord, and from the *macarons* of Saint Emilion, in Bordeaux, made with honey, almonds, and Sauternes wine, to babas and savarins drenched with kirsch from Alsace. The Paris Lenôtre shops offer these *pâtisseries* and many other regional treats on an occasional basis, and always to order, reviving interest among Paris gourmands in France's great culinary repertoire of provincial desserts.

The head of this global gastronomic empire began life very simply on a large, thriving farm in Normandy, which had been purchased by his father, Gaston, once the sous-chef at the Grand Hotel in Paris, and his mother, Eléonore, who had also worked in Paris as an apprentice cook. Gaston junior and his younger brother Marcel, also a *pâtissier*, share memories of golden *gâteau de riz*, silky *crème caramels*, and *petit-sablés* shortbread cookies, their first childhood pastries prepared by their mother from Normandy's rich butter and thick, heavy creams. In 1947, after many years of training followed by the dark pall of World War II, Gaston Lenôtre and his wife, Colette,

opened their first *pâtisserie* in the small Norman town of Pont-Audemer, a short drive east from Deauville. After ten successful years at their Norman shop, they made the decision to try their luck in Paris, opening a shop at 44 rue d'Auteuil in the fashionable sixteenth arrondissement, still the flagship boutique. *"L'aventure Parisienne,"* as Monsieur Lenôtre likes to say, had begun.

In a career that spans more than half a century, from the early provincial years to the multinational domain of today, Gaston Lenôtre has been an imaginative and farsighted innovator responsible for major changes in the character and content of French *pâtisserie*. While hardly dietetic, and still dependent on butter, sugar, and cream, the *pâtisserie* of today is cloudlike in comparison to the denser confections of even fifty years ago. Early in his career, Monsieur Lenôtre began his efforts to lighten and refine his *pâtisserie*, reducing the butter in his *pâte feuilletée* and other pastry doughs, cutting back on the use of rich, heavy *crème pâtissières* as basic fillings, and experimenting with the use of

fruits—once consigned almost exclusively to tarts—as a central component in mousses, cream fillings, and bases. The lightness, freshness, and refinement of Paris *pâtisserie* today is in large measure due to the innovations of Gaston Lenôtre. Along the way, as he baked his way to a success far beyond his dreams, he became *une star*, not only in gastronomic circles, but in the public domain as well. Many of today's top *pâtissiers* and *boulangers* readily admit that their own visibility, even celebrity, would not have been possible without the prestige that Gaston Lenôtre has brought to the image of French *pâtisserie*.

To perpetuate the grand traditions and techniques of French *pâtisserie* and cuisine, Gaston Lenôtre opened the Ecole de Gastronomie Lenôtre at Plaisir in 1971, primarily for professional chefs, but now offering courses for amateur cooks as well. In a métier where trade secrets are often jealously guarded, Monsieur Lenôtre has been unusually generous and paternal in sharing his knowledge and the secrets of his success to disciples whom he describes as future

FROM THE RUE D'AUTEUIL, THE WINDOW OF LENÔTRE'S FIRST PARIS SHOP
TANTALIZES WITH AN ARRAY OF COLORFUL PASTRIES.

ambassadors of French taste, so that they can spread the gospel of French gastronomy to the four corners of the world. These days Gaston Lenôtre, having earned himself the position of a living legend, travels the world, lectures at the school, oversees operations at two elegant restaurants he now owns in Paris, and between engagements, enjoys an exquisitely prepared morsel of *pâtisserie* as much as ever. After a lifetime in *pâtisserie,* one wonders, is there a secret to staying slim and energetic well into one's seventies? "Well, yes, I suppose I have two secrets," he confides. "Every morning when I wake up, I start my day with a *tisane*—an 'herb tea'—of garlic and thyme. And after every lunch and dinner I eat a fresh lemon!" Pastry lovers take note: With the Lenôtre nostrum, perhaps we have, at last, the antidote to indulgence!

❋

Paris-Brest

....

The name Paris-Brest refers to an old French bicycle race between two cities, starting in the capital and ending in Brittany. To commemorate the annual event, this classic pastry was created in 1891 to look like a large bicycle wheel. If you can't get praline paste, flavor the cream with a little more rum, coffee, or Grand Marnier.

½ RECIPE PATE À CHOUX
(PAGE 147)

1 LARGE EGG YOLK, BEATEN WITH
½ TEASPOON COLD WATER

2 TABLESPOONS SLICED OR
CHOPPED BLANCHED ALMONDS

....

CRÈME PARIS-BREST (FILLING)

½ CUP (1 STICK) PLUS
2 TABLESPOONS/150 G UNSALTED
BUTTER, AT COOL ROOM
TEMPERATURE

¼ CUP PLUS 1 TABLESPOON/80 G
PRALINE PASTE OR POWDER
(SEE MAIL-ORDER SOURCES,
PAGE 155)

CREATED A CENTURY AGO IN THE SHAPE OF A WHEEL TO COMMEMORATE A BICYCLE RACE, THE PARIS-BREST IS A RING OF ALMOND-TOPPED CHOUX PASTRY FILLED WITH PRALINE-FLAVORED CREAM.

....

½ RECIPE PASTRY CREAM
(PAGE 146), COLD

1 TEASPOON RUM OR COGNAC
(OR INSTANT COFFEE DISSOLVED
IN HOT WATER)

CONFECTIONERS' SUGAR, FOR
SPRINKLING

Preheat the oven to 425°F./220°C. Line a baking sheet with parchment paper or butter and flour the sheet.

Spoon the *pâte à choux* into a pastry bag fitted with a ½-inch/1-cm plain tip, or use the bag without a tip. With a pencil, and using a cake pan or plate as a guide, trace an 8-inch/20-cm circle on the paper to guide you. Pipe 3 rings of dough: First, form an 8-inch/20-cm ring of dough, following the pencil mark. Next, form a second ring within the first ring, touching the inner edge of the first ring. Then, form a third, high ring, "piggyback" on top of and between the first 2 rings.

Gently brush the surface of the dough with the yolk glaze, then scatter the almonds over the surface.

Bake the pastry for 10 minutes, or until it has puffed and is lightly golden. Lower the oven temperature to 350°F./175°C. and bake until the pastry is golden brown, about 30

minutes longer. Prop the oven door slightly ajar with the handle of a wooden spoon and leave the pastry in the oven for 15 minutes longer, keeping the oven at 350°F./175°C. to help dry out the pastry. Remove from the oven and cool the pan on a wire rack.

When the pastry has cooled completely, use a long serrated knife to neatly cut off the top of the pastry, making the cut at the base of the top ring and reserving the top.

CRÈME PARIS-BREST (FILLING): The pastry should be filled as close to serving time as possible. Beat the butter in a mixing bowl with the heel of your hand, or in an electric mixer with the whisk attachment. The butter should be soft enough to be malleable but still somewhat firm and cool. When the butter is smooth, add the praline paste, mixing with a hand-held electric mixer, or the mixer with a whisk attachment, until combined. Gradually add the pastry cream, then whip slowly for 2 minutes to lighten the mixture. Add the rum or coffee.

Spoon the *crème Paris-Brest* into a pastry bag with a 1-inch/2-cm star tip.

GASTON LENÔTRE, THE KING OF FRENCH PÂTISSIERS, SURVEYS HIS REALM ON THE RUE D'AUTEUIL IN PARIS.

Place the pastry ring on a platter lined with a doily. Pipe the cream into the pastry ring, letting it come up above the edges of the pastry and forming rosettes or flames around the edges. Gently replace the top of the pastry over the cream and refrigerate until serving time. (The pastry should be filled no more than 1 hour before serving if possible. If the cream has firmed up in the refrigerator, take it out about 20 minutes before serving.) Sprinkle the top of the pastry with confectioners' sugar. Cut in wedges and serve.

SERVES ABOUT 8

✽

Savarin au Chantilly

....

This savarin is a variation of the classic circular Baba au Rhum.

Monsieur Lenôtre notes that the baked savarin can be frozen. While it is still slightly lukewarm (before moistening with syrup), wrap the cake tightly in plastic, enclose in a plastic bag, and freeze for up to 2 months. To defrost, leave the cake in the refrigerator for 24 hours, then soak with syrup and glaze as directed.

YEAST DOUGH

2 TEASPOONS DRY YEAST

2 TABLESPOONS LUKEWARM
WATER

3 TABLESPOONS MILK, PLUS
MORE AS NEEDED

1 ¾ CUPS/250 G ALL-PURPOSE
FLOUR

1 TEASPOON SALT

2 LARGE EGGS

1 LARGE EGG YOLK

1 TABLESPOON SUGAR

5 TABLESPOONS/75 G UNSALTED
BUTTER, MELTED AND COOLED
SLIGHTLY

....

SIROP AU RHUM (RUM SYRUP)

1 ½ CUPS/300 G SUGAR

2 CUPS/500 ML COLD WATER

2 TABLESPOONS RUM
OR KIRSCH

....

GARNISH

⅓ CUP/100 G APRICOT JAM,
OR AS NEEDED

1 CUP/250 ML HEAVY CREAM,
WELL CHILLED

CANDIED ORANGE SLIVERS OR
CHOCOLATE SHAVINGS
(OPTIONAL)

YEAST DOUGH: In the bowl of an electric mixer, or in a large bowl, dissolve the yeast in the lukewarm water and milk; let stand for 5 or 10 minutes. Add the flour and salt, and slowly begin to mix the ingredients together with the dough hook attachment or by hand with a wooden spoon. Raise the mixer speed to medium; add 1 egg and the yolk and mix at least 1 minute or stir vigorously by hand, until the ingredients have come together to form a firm dough. Scrape the mixture from the sides of the bowl and the beaters or the spoon, as needed. Add the remaining egg and continue to mix until the mixture is smooth and elastic, about 5 minutes.

Add the sugar, then the melted butter, mixing until the dough is very soft, smooth, and elastic. If necessary, drizzle in a little more milk. Knead the dough at least 2 minutes longer. When you pull at the dough with your fingers, it should stretch without breaking. Cover the dough and let it rest in a warm draft-free place for 20 minutes. Don't let the dough rise too much at this stage, or the cake will be too fragile.

Lightly butter a ring mold about 8 inches/20 cm in diameter or use a *kugelhopf* mold. Punch the dough down and arrange it evenly in the bottom of the mold. Cover and let rise in a warm draft-free place until it reaches the rim of the pan, about 1½ hours. (With an 8-inch/20-cm *kugelhopf* mold, the dough will only come up about three-quarters full.)

Preheat the oven to 400°F./ 200°C. Bake the baba for 25 minutes, or until a knife blade inserted in the center comes out dry. Unmold the cake onto a wire rack over a jelly roll pan or large plate. Cool completely.

SIROP AU RHUM (RUM SYRUP): Bring the sugar and water to a boil over medium-high heat, stirring to dissolve the sugar. Cool to lukewarm, then add the rum. With a ladle, slowly pour the syrup all over the cake, until it has absorbed most of the syrup, reserving ½ cup/125 ml for serving. The center should be soft when pressed. Carefully transfer the baba to a serving platter. Set aside at room temperature, unwrapped, if serving within 2 hours. Or refrigerate, loosely wrapped, until 1 hour before serving.

Just before serving, spoon a little more syrup over the cake. Heat the apricot jam over low heat until melted. Strain the jam into a small bowl or measuring cup and brush the surface of the cake with the jam.

Whip the cream until nearly stiff. Spoon it gently into a pastry bag fitted with a large (¾-inch/ 2-cm) star tip. Pipe the whipped cream into the center of the baba, forming large rosettes. Garnish with slivers of candied orange or chocolate shavings. Cut the baba into wedges with a serrated knife and serve some of the whipped cream with each portion.

SERVES 8 TO 10

✽

Tarte aux Noix

....

[WALNUT TART]

....

This rustic nut tart recipe originates in the Périgord, a region in southwestern France where walnuts are an important crop. As a distinctive counterpoint to the walnuts, the recipe calls for either Grand Marnier or strong coffee. Either flavor gives the tart real character.

1 RECIPE PÂTE SUCRÉE DOUGH,
CHILLED (PAGE 28).

....

THE TARTE AUX NOIX, LENÔTRE'S RUSTIC WALNUT TART INSPIRED BY A TRADITIONAL RECIPE FROM
THE PÉRIGORD, IS A DISTANT FRENCH COUSIN TO THE PECAN PIE.

. . . .

WALNUT FILLING

2 LARGE EGGS

¹/₂ CUP PLUS 2 TABLESPOONS/
70 G GRANULATED SUGAR

¹/₃ CUP/100 G CRÈME FRAÎCHE
OR HEAVY CREAM

¹/₂ CUP (SCANT)/120 ML
GRAND MARNIER OR VERY
STRONG COFFEE

3 TABLESPOONS/45 G UNSALTED
BUTTER, SOFTENED

³/₈ CUP/75 G BROWN SUGAR

2 ¹/₃ CUPS/200 G CHOPPED
WALNUTS

. . . .

GARNISH

CONFECTIONERS' SUGAR,
FOR SPRINKLING

8 TO 10 WHOLE WALNUT PIECES

Roll the chilled *pâte sucrée* pastry on a lightly floured sheet of wax paper or plastic wrap into a 13-inch/33-cm circle about ¹/₈ inch/¹/₃ cm thick, lightly dusting the pastry with flour as needed. Chill the pastry briefly to make it easier to handle. Carefully invert the pastry, wax paper–side up, onto a buttered 10- or 11-inch/25- or 28-cm false-bottomed tart pan, fitting it without stretching and pressing the dough to fit the fluted sides of the pan. Carefully peel off the wax paper and trim the edges. You can also fit the pastry into a buttered 9-inch/23-cm springform pan, forming even sides about 1¹/₂ inches/4 cm high. Refrigerate the pastry shell for at least ¹/₂ hour.

Preheat the oven to 375°F./190°C. Place the tart pan in a jelly roll pan or on a baking sheet. Line the pastry shell with parchment paper or lightly buttered aluminum foil and fill with dried beans or rice. Bake for 15 minutes; then carefully remove the beans and foil and bake 5 minutes longer, or until the pastry is pale gold. Remove from the oven, turning the oven temperature up to 425°F./220°C.

WALNUT FILLING: In a medium mixing bowl, beat together the eggs, sugar, and crème fraîche with a wooden spoon. Add the Grand Marnier, the butter, brown sugar, and chopped nuts, mixing well until all the ingredients are blended. Carefully pour the filling into the shell. Lower the oven temperature to 375°F./190°C. and bake 40 to 45 minutes, until the top is golden brown. Cool on a rack. Sprinkle lightly with confectioners' sugar and decorate the top with the whole walnut pieces, pressed lightly into the filling. Serve at room temperature.

MAKES 8 SERVINGS

A WIDE CHOICE OF CRUSTY BREADS AND ROLLS ARE AMONG THE GREAT VARIETY OF BAKED GOODS CHEZ LENÔTRE.

A BASKETFUL OF GANACHAUD'S FAMOUS "FLÛTES" COOLS BEFORE BEING DELIVERED TO NEARBY RESTAURANTS.

Pain au Son

....

Tarte Normande

....

Gâteaux de Riz

....

Croissants aux Amandes

....

Clafoutis aux Cerises

....

Pain Brioché

GANACHAUD

It was the neighborhood of Chevalier, Mistinguett, Piaf, and Signoret, the twentieth arrondissement, a sprawling *quartier populaire,* inhabited primarily by working-class families and newly arrived immigrants. Beyond the somber attraction of the huge Père Lachaise cemetery, final resting place of Colette, Chopin, Proust, and Jim Morrison, among others, there was little reason to trek up here to the northern reaches of Paris. But that was before Bernard Ganachaud, a master baker from Nantes whose father and grandfather were bakers before him, set up shop over thirty years ago on the ground floor of a government-subsidized apartment complex on the rue Ménilmontant. Here Ganachaud began baking a panoply of wondrous breads the likes of which most Parisians had never tasted. The delicious, distinctive loaves that emerged from his wood-fired ovens were the products of both old family recipes and new ones Monsieur Ganachaud had developed himself. His reputation spread so quickly that bread lovers began leaving their arrondissements—and later even their suburbs—to beat a path to his brick-fronted shop. For a while even the exclusive Hôtel Crillon was sending an emissary in a taxi to bring back Ganachaud breads for their tables. There are many in this city of gourmands who believe that Ganachaud simply makes the best bread in Paris.

For the quality of his products and his contributions to his métier, in 1979 Bernard Ganachaud earned the prestigious Meilleur Ouvrier de France award,

BERNARD GANACHAUD IS THE PROUD PAPA OF DAUGHTERS VALÉRIE, LEFT,
AND ISABELLE, RIGHT, WHO PERPETUATE THE FAMILY BAKING TRADITION
WITH THEIR BOULANGERIE, LA FLÛTE GANA.

presented each year by the government to the country's top artisans. The bread that has drawn the most acclaim is Ganachaud's signature whole wheat baguette, La Flûte Gana, a unique blend of stone-ground flours with the subtle taste of hazelnuts. The "Flûte," as well as many of the other breads chez Ganachaud, undergo particularly long fermentations resulting in unusually rich grain flavor. Ganachaud employs a technique called *"sur poolish,"* a turn-of-the-century method of preparing the dough using a starter of flour, water, and yeast prepared at least six hours before the *pétrissage*, the final mixing and kneading of the dough.

But the taste is only part of the bread's appeal.

"The perfect baguette must please all the senses," says the dynamic, white-haired Monsieur Ganachaud, with the intensity that comes into his voice whenever the subject is bread. "For the eye, the exterior must be golden brown, with even

lames or cuts diagonally across the top, the interior swelling slightly through; the *mie,* or crumb of the bread—the inside—must have a variety of large, small, and medium holes—*alvéoles*—from a good fermentation. For the ears the bread must be *croustillon,* crispy, emitting a delicate crackle when you squeeze it lightly. To the touch the crust must be slightly resistant, like an eggshell, not soft. For the nose, the bread must emit a tantalizing, savory aroma. And to the taste, the essence of the grain must come through."

After a lifetime of hard work that began when he was eight years old, helping out his father before and after school, Bernard Ganachaud, now in his mid-sixties, is taking life a little easier. The original Ganachaud enterprise, on the rue Ménilmontant, has recently been sold to a baker-colleague, who continues to run it under the Ganachaud name and to the Ganachaud standards. This leaves Monsieur Ganachaud free to lecture, travel

throughout the world, often with his wife Josette, study, and frequently look in on La Flûte Gana, the shop he opened with his daughters, Isabelle and Valérie, on the rue des Pyrénées. The three baking Ganachauds have also inaugurated a group of small boutique franchises of La Flûte Gana in Japan, spreading the gospel of great artisanal French breads to the Orient.

In the male-dominated world of French *boulange*—the baking of bread—the sisters Ganachaud are unique. When they graduated together at the top of their class from the rigorous Institut National de la Boulangerie in Rouen, earning the respected title of *Maître en Boulangerie,* or Master Baker, as their father did almost forty years earlier, they became not only the first pair of sisters to achieve such a level of expertise, but also the only women. Interestingly, too, baking was the second career for both sisters: Isabelle had had a previous career as a nurse and Valérie as an office administrator. The change was spurred by the fear that upon their

A SIDEWALK SIGN ADVERTISES BREAD
COOKED IN A WOOD-FIRED OVEN.

father's downshift into third gear from years of operating in overdrive, the Ganachaud dynasty would end. "My daughters," Bernard Ganachaud says simply, "have brought me extraordinary happiness."

An intensely loyal and complementary duo, Isabelle and Valérie lead a feisty team of bakers and apprentices who turn out up to thirty varieties of bread daily as well as rustic, home-style pastries. All of their products are *artisanale*, created entirely by hand, using classic recipes, market-fresh ingredients, and stone-ground, custom-blended flours. "The *boulangerie* is a passion, absolutely," says Isabelle. "The work is too hard, the hours too long to choose to do it without loving it. But the satisfactions are great—the look, the smell, the texture of a fine bread, and the pleasure it brings to people. When I see the face of a tired worker light up with a smile as he inhales the aroma of our warm baguette that he's bought for his dinner, well, it's all really worth it."

❋

Pain au Son

. . . .

[DIETETIC BRAN BREAD]

. . . .

This bread, almost half of which is wheat bran, is sold in many bakeries as *pain de régime*, or diet bread.

2 TEASPOONS (ABOUT ³/₄ ENVE-
LOPE)/5 G DRY YEAST

2³/₄ CUPS/700 G LUKEWARM
WATER

5¹/₄ CUPS (1 ¹/₂ POUNDS)/
750 G ALL-PURPOSE FLOUR

2¹/₄ CUPS (7 OUNCES)/
200 G WHEAT BRAN

4 TEASPOONS SALT

In a measuring cup, sprinkle the yeast over 2 tablespoons of the lukewarm water; set aside for 10 minutes. Combine the flour with the bran on a work surface or in the bowl of an electric mixer fitted with a dough hook. Make a well in the center of

PAIN AU SON IS POPULAR EVEN
AMONG PARISIANS WHO DON'T HAVE
TO WATCH THEIR WEIGHT.

. . . .

the flour mixture and add the salt, the yeast mixture, and the remaining lukewarm water. Gradually incorporate the dry ingredients into the wet. When the dough begins to come together, cut the mixture several times, pinching it between your thumbs and index fingers, then gathering the dough back toward you. If you are using the machine, simply mix until the dough becomes homogeneous.

When the dough begins to offer some resistance, lift a portion of the dough, stretching it, then let it fall back on itself. Repeat several times, which will incorporate air into the dough. When the dough is ready, it will not stick to your hands. Place the dough in an oiled bowl, cover with a damp kitchen towel, and let rise in a draft-free place for 1¹/₂ hours, or until it has doubled in volume.

Punch the dough down, pushing the edges of the dough toward the center. Cover and let rise again for 30 minutes, or refrigerate overnight. Butter an 8 x 4-inch/20 x 10-cm loaf pan. Pat the dough to a rectangle roughly the same length as the pan.

Starting with a long side, fold the dough into thirds and gently lay it into the pan; it should be nearly two-thirds full. Cover again with a damp towel and let rise until the dough comes up to the rim of the pan, about 1 hour or slightly longer. Moisten the surface of the dough with a brush dipped in water.

Preheat the oven to 375°F./ 190°C., with a rack slightly below center level. Bake the bread for about 50 minutes, or until it is golden brown and the bottom sounds hollow when tapped. Brush the surface again with water, invert onto a wire rack, and cool. Cut and serve the bread the following day. To keep, wrap the bread in a clean cloth or plastic bag and refrigerate.

MAKES TWO 8-INCH/
20-CM LOAVES

❋

Tarte Normande ✓

. . . .

[NORMANDY APPLE AND
CUSTARD TART]

. . . .

Monsieur Ganachaud notes that the quality of the apples is of prime importance in this recipe. He prefers la Reine des Reinettes apples, which are sweet and firm. Golden Delicious apples also work well, and are available throughout the year.

1 DOUBLE RECIPE (12 OUNCES)
PÂTE SUCRÉE (PAGE 28)
OR 12 OUNCES/360 G PURCHASED
PUFF PASTRY (OR USE THE
RECIPE ON PAGE 116, CHILLED)

. . . .

FILLING

2 LARGE EGGS

2 LARGE EGG WHITES

¹/₄ CUP/50 G SUGAR, PLUS MORE
AS NEEDED

¹/₂ CUP/125 ML CREME FRAICHE
OR HEAVY CREAM

2 CUPS/500 ML MILK

3 OR 4 GOLDEN DELICIOUS
APPLES, PEELED, HALVED,
CORED, HALVED CROSSWISE, AND
SLICED THIN

TARTES NORMANDES, RUSTIC APPLE TARTS FROM LA FLÛTE GANA, EXEMPLIFY THE BOULANGER'S UNCOMPLICATED APPROACH TO PASTRY.

. . . .

Butter 8 tartlet pans. (This recipe will make about eight 4-inch/10-cm tartlets, ten to twelve 3-inch/8-cm tartlets, or two 8-inch/20-cm tarts. You can also bake these in a muffin tin; do not use a dark metal pan, or the pastry will brown too quickly.) Roll out the pastry on a lightly floured work surface to a thickness of slightly less than $\frac{1}{8}$ inch/$1\frac{1}{3}$ cm. Using an appropriately sized cutter or saucer as a guide, cut out rounds of pastry and fit them without stretching into the pans, so that the pastry comes up slightly higher than the rims of the pans. Chill the pastry, uncovered, overnight, or for at least 1 hour.

FILLING: In a large mixing bowl, whisk the eggs, egg whites, and sugar until well blended. Add the cream, whisking until smooth. Add the milk and whisk until smooth.

Preheat the oven to 400°F./200°C. Place the tart sheets about 1 inch/ 2 $\frac{1}{2}$ cm apart on a foil-lined baking sheet to catch any drips. Sprinkle the surface of the tart shells lightly with sugar. Arrange the apple slices in an overlapping circle over the pastry. Gently pour the filling over the apples without disturbing them.

Bake the tarts until the custard has set (the custard is firm in the center when the pan is jiggled), about 35 minutes (timing can vary based on the size and depth of the pans; do not overbake). Remove the pans from the sheet and cool on a wire rack, then serve at cool room temperature. Refrigerate the tarts, covered, if holding longer than a couple of hours, taking them out of the refrigerator about 15 minutes before serving. These tarts are best served on the day they are baked.

MAKES ABOUT EIGHT 4-INCH/ 10-CM TARTLETS

❋

Gâteaux de Riz

. . . .

[GOLDEN RICE TARTLETS]

. . . .

Bernard Ganachaud bakes these custardy tartlets in deep oval molds. At home, the easiest method is to bake them in a muffin tin, preferably not one made of dark metal, which will brown the pastry too quickly. Individual molds or ramekins will also work fine. Note that, based on the size and depth of the molds you use, the yield will vary slightly and the baking time may need to be adjusted.

1 DOUBLE RECIPE PÂTE SUCRÉE
(PAGE 28) OR PUFF PASTRY,
EITHER HOMEMADE USING
HALF THE RECIPE ON PAGE 116
OR PURCHASED

. . . .

FILLING

3 CUPS/750 ML MILK

$\frac{1}{2}$ VANILLA BEAN, SPLIT
LENGTHWISE, OR 2 TEASPOONS
VANILLA EXTRACT

$\frac{1}{4}$ CUP PLUS 1 TABLESPOON/
75 G UNCOOKED LONG-
GRAIN RICE

PINCH OF SALT

5 TABLESPOONS/75 G UNSALTED
BUTTER, CUT INTO PIECES

3 LARGE EGGS

$\frac{1}{4}$ CUP PLUS 1 TABLESPOON/
75 G SUGAR

Butter individual deep oval or round tartlet molds, or a muffin tin with 3-inch/8-cm cups that hold about $\frac{1}{2}$ cup each. Roll out the pastry on a lightly floured work surface to a thickness of slightly less than $\frac{1}{8}$ inch/$\frac{1}{3}$ cm. Using a 4-inch/10-cm cutter or saucer, cut rounds of pastry and fit them without stretching into the cups. The edges of the pastry should be slightly higher than the rims of the pan. Chill the pastry, uncovered, for at least 1 hour.

FILLING: Combine the milk, vanilla, rice, and salt in a heavy saucepan. Bring to a boil over medium-high heat, then lower the heat and simmer gently, uncovered, stirring very frequently, until the liquid has been absorbed, about 30 minutes. Stir often and watch carefully toward the end of the cooking time to prevent burning. Remove from the heat and stir in the butter until it has melted. In a large mixing bowl, whisk the eggs and sugar until well mixed. Slowly add a few spoonfuls of the hot rice to the eggs, stirring vigorously. Stir the remainder of the rice into the eggs until combined.

Preheat the oven to 375°F./ 190°C. Pour the rice filling into the pastry-lined cups, filling them about four-fifths full. Bake until the filling has set and is lightly golden, 30 to 35 minutes (the timing can vary based on the depth of the molds; do not overbake). Check the tarts occasionally as they bake; if the tops begin to brown before the custard has set, lay a sheet of aluminum foil over the tarts and continue to bake until they are set. Cool the pan briefly on a wire rack; then gently unmold the tartlets, running a knife gently around the edges of the pastry, and remove from the pan. Cool the tartlets completely and serve at cool room temperature. The tartlets can be covered and refrigerated, removing about $\frac{1}{2}$ hour before serving.

MAKES ABOUT FOURTEEN
3-INCH/8-CM TARTLETS

GOLDEN, EGGY, AND DENSE WITH RICE, THESE GÂTEAUX DE RIZ ARE CREATED FROM AN OLD GANACHAUD FAMILY RECIPE.

KIRSCH-FLAVORED CROISSANTS AUX AMANDES ARE A LUSCIOUS WAY TO RECYCLE DAY-OLD CROISSANTS.

Croissants aux Amandes

....

[ALMOND-FILLED CROISSANTS]

....

A great way to recycle day-or-two-old croissants, this recipe with almonds and kirsch will also give flavor and fresh-baked character to commercially produced fresh or frozen croissants.

SIROP PÂTISSIER (SUGAR SYRUP)

$^{1}/_{3}$ CUP/70 ML WATER

$^{1}/_{2}$ CUP/100 G SUGAR

2 TABLESPOONS KIRSCH

....

CRÈME D'AMANDES (ALMOND CREAM)

$^{2}/_{3}$ CUP/150 G SUGAR

10 TABLESPOONS
(1 $^{1}/_{4}$ STICKS)/150 G UNSALTED
BUTTER

$^{3}/_{4}$ CUP/142 G POWDERED
ALMONDS

2 LARGE EGGS

2 TABLESPOONS KIRSCH

8 CROISSANTS, 1 OR 2 DAYS OLD

$^{2}/_{3}$ CUP/60 G SLICED ALMONDS

CONFECTIONERS' SUGAR,
FOR DUSTING

SIROP PÂTISSIER (SUGAR SYRUP): Combine the water and sugar in a small saucepan. Bring to a boil over medium heat, stirring frequently to dissolve all the sugar. Remove from the heat and let cool. Add the kirsch and stir to blend. Set aside.

CRÈME D'AMANDES (ALMOND CREAM): In a medium bowl, cream the sugar and butter together until the mixture turns smooth and pale. Add the powdered almonds and mix until blended. Then beat the eggs in one at a time, mixing until the batter is golden and creamy. Add the kirsch and mix until blended.

ASSEMBLY: Preheat the oven to 400°F./200°C. Split the croissants lengthwise and lay them on a lightly buttered cookie sheet. With a pastry brush, generously baste both sides of the croissants with the *sirop pâtissier*. With a small spatula, spread the

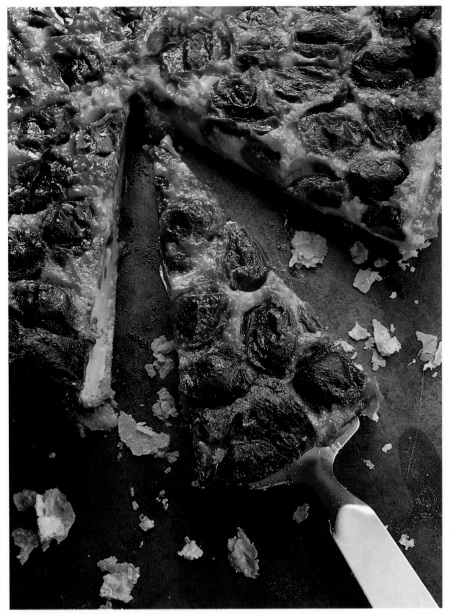

A RUSTIC, FLANLIKE DESSERT, THE CLAFOUTIS AUX CERISES, CHERRY CLAFOUTIS, ORIGINATED IN THE LIMOUSIN REGION OF SOUTHWEST FRANCE.

....

crème d'amandes onto the interior sides of the croissants, reserving about one-quarter of the mixture to spread over the tops. Sprinkle about two-thirds of the sliced almonds over the interior sides. Close the croissants. Spread the remaining almond cream over the tops, then sprinkle on the remaining almonds. Dust the croissants with confectioners' sugar. Bake for about 10 minutes, until the almond topping turns deep golden brown. Let cool slightly on the cookie sheet before serving.

MAKES 8 SERVINGS

Clafoutis aux Cerises

....

[CHERRY CLAFOUTIS]

....

This rustic, flanlike dessert, traditionally made with black cherries, is prepared in a pastry shell chez Ganachaud. The recipe works equally well with a variety of other fruits—a mixture of apples and prunes; fresh pears, plums, peaches, or apricots. It is delicious served slightly warm with a side of crème fraîche.

3 CUPS/750 ML MILK

1¼ CUPS/250 G SUGAR

1 VANILLA BEAN, SPLIT
LENGTHWISE, OR 1 TEASPOON
VANILLA EXTRACT

⅔ CUP/100 G ALL-PURPOSE
FLOUR

5 LARGE EGGS

1 UNBAKED 10½-INCH/
26½-CM PURCHASED PÂTE FEUIL-
LETÉ TART SHELL, OR USE THE
RECIPE ON PAGE 116

1½ POUNDS/625 G PITTED
RIPE CHERRIES

CONFECTIONERS' SUGAR,
FOR SPRINKLING

Preheat the oven to 400°F./200°C. In a heavy medium saucepan, combine the milk, sugar, and vanilla bean or vanilla extract. Bring to a boil, stirring constantly to dissolve the sugar. Reduce the heat to low and simmer for 2 to 3 minutes. Remove from the heat and let cool to lukewarm.

Measure the flour into a large mixing bowl. With an electric mixer on medium speed or stirring vigorously by hand, add the eggs one at a time, blending after each addition and scraping down the sides of the bowl frequently. The batter should be smooth with no lumps. Remove the vanilla bean from the milk mixture and gradually pour the milk into the egg mixture, beating constantly until blended. The mixture will be quite thin.

Pour the batter into the prepared tart shell, filling it three-quarters full. Arrange the cherries evenly over the top of the batter. If the filling does not quite rise up to the top of the pastry crust, top it off with remaining batter. Bake for 50 to 60 minutes, until puffed and golden brown. Cool on a rack until lukewarm, then sprinkle the top generously with confectioners' sugar, remove the sides of the pan, and serve in wedges.

MAKES 6 TO 8 SERVINGS

Note: *Clafoutis* is generally prepared without a crust. Ganachaud's

clafoutis is also delicious—and slightly less caloric—baked on its own in a well-buttered ceramic baking dish or pie plate.

❋

Pain Brioché

[BRIOCHE BREAD]

BRIOCHE DOUGH

2 TABLESPOONS LUKEWARM
WATER

2 TEASPOONS (ABOUT ¾ ENVE-
LOPE) DRY YEAST

4 CUPS/500 G ALL-PURPOSE
FLOUR

¾ CUP/175 ML MILK

1½ TEASPOONS SALT

2 LARGE EGGS

1½ TEASPOONS VANILLA
SUGAR, OR USE 1½ TEASPOONS
SUGAR AND ¾ TEASPOON
VANILLA EXTRACT

½ CUP (1 STICK)/125 G UNSALT-
ED BUTTER, SOFTENED

¼ CUP PLUS 3 TABLESPOONS/
90 G SUGAR

GLAZE

1 LARGE EGG, WELL-BEATEN

1½ TABLESPOONS/25 G UNSALT-
ED BUTTER, MELTED

BRIOCHE DOUGH: Place the lukewarm water in a measuring cup, sprinkle with the yeast, and set aside, for 10 minutes. Place the flour on a work surface or in the bowl of an electric mixer fitted with a dough hook. Heat the milk to lukewarm over low heat. Make a well in the center of the flour; add the yeast mixture, the lukewarm milk, salt, eggs, and vanilla sugar. Begin to mix the dough with your fingers (or with the dough hook at slow speed), pinching the mixture between your thumbs and index fingers until it comes together. Mix until the dough is smooth.

In a small bowl, combine the butter and sugar, stirring steadily

until the mixture is smooth and pale yellow. With the dough still in the mixing bowl or set in a large buttered bowl if the dough was mixed on a work surface, add the butter mixture to the dough in small increments, about 2 tablespoons at a time. As you add the butter mixture, pinch the dough between your fingertips, incorporating the butter into the dough. Then pick up the dough, stretching it upward from the bottom of the bowl. Continue to add more butter mixture, pinching, then stretching after each addition, until the butter mixture is completely incorporated and the dough is smooth, elastic, and sticky. Form the dough into a ball, set it in the center of the mixing bowl, cover with a damp kitchen towel, and set aside in a draft-free place until the dough has doubled in volume, about 1¾ hours. Punch the dough down or fold it over onto itself. Cover again with plastic wrap and refrigerate overnight.

The next day, remove the dough from the refrigerator and let stand in the bowl at room temperature for 1 hour. Then divide the dough into 4 equal portions, and form each into a ball slightly less than 4 inches/10 cm wide. Place 2 balls in each of 2 buttered 8 x 4-inch/20 x 10-cm loaf pans, 1 ball at each end of the pan. The dough should come up one-third to one-half the height of the pan. Cover and let rise to the rim of the pan. The dough will expand to fill the pan, creating a "2-humped" loaf with a seam in the middle. Lightly brush the surface of the dough with the beaten egg.

Preheat the oven to 350°F./175°C. Bake 40 to 45 minutes, until the loaf is golden brown and sounds hollow when tapped on the bottom. Just after the bread comes out of the oven, brush the surface with the melted butter. Place on a wire rack and cool for 1 hour.

MAKES TWO 8-INCH/
20-CM LOAVES

PAIN BRIOCHÉ IS DELICIOUS TOASTED FOR BREAKFAST, WITH JAM AT TEA-TIME, OR WITH FOIE GRAS AT DINNER.

HOT FROM THE OVEN, HAUPOIS'S TEMPTING CROISSANTS COOL ON THEIR BAKING RACKS.

Croquets Bourbonnais
....
Pains au Raisins
....
Croissants · Gougères
....
La Galette (Baguette Aplati)
....
Pain de Campagne

The Ile-St.-Louis sits in the middle of the Seine like a permanently moored ocean liner, solitary and splendid. The sense of being a place apart, a village unto itself, pervades the Ile-St.-Louis. The residents refer to themselves as *insulaires*—connoting the fact that they are actual islanders, removed in a physical way from the city's Right and Left Banks. Spending time here—perhaps staying for several nights in one of the three small hotels on the rue St.-Louis-en-Ile—you get a sense of the village life that still characterizes the *île,* though perhaps less so than in the twenties and thirties when some *insulaires* liked to boast that they only "went to Paris" to be born, to marry, and to be interred.

The rue des Deux-Ponts—the Street of the Two Bridges—runs through the center of the island, linking the Ile-St.-Louis to both the Right and the Left banks by the Pont Marie and the Pont de la Tournelle. Once a street of artisans and modest service establishments—shoemakers, ironmongers, laundries, and the paint shop where former resident Marc Chagall bought his supplies—it is now dominated by boutiques, restaurants, and real estate offices. One exception can be found behind the old oak facade at #35, simply marked "Boulangerie," where Marcel Haupois has been turning out delicious croissants, country breads, and *gâteaux boulangers*—"bakers' cakes"—for more than thirty years. This simple shop with a strikingly elaborate ceiling mural

LOOKING ONTO THE RUE DES DEUX PONTS, THE BAKERY'S WINDOW HAS BEEN
DISPLAYING EDIBLE WARES FOR MORE THAN 100 YEARS.

. . . .

has existed for more than a century and is the archetype of the Paris neighborhood bakery. Monsieur Haupois's more than thirty varieties of wonderfully crusty, chewy loaves are among the best in Paris. Bread lovers adore his unusual *galette,* or *baguette aplati* (literally "flattened baguette"), a discus-shaped loaf of baguette dough that is almost completely crust, developed for those who much prefer the outside of the baguette over the *mie,* or interior, of the bread. (I once had two roommates when I first lived in Paris. One girl would only eat the crust of the baguette; the other girl would only eat the soft, white *mie;* I ate both. We had a very happy *ménage* with never a crumb left over.)

Neighborhood *insulaires* stand patiently in line in the morning to buy Monsieur Haupois's big, flaky croissants and golden, round *pains aux raisins*—sweet raisin buns— from the vigilant Madame Haupois, Renée, who runs the front of the shop. Toward noontime the line of buyers awaits the warm-from-the-oven breads, especially the baguettes. "In spite of the great variety of

breads available here and elsewhere in Paris," the energetic, bespectacled Monsieur Haupois remarks, "it is the baguette, which originated in Paris around the turn of the century, that is still the most popular bread. It is bread you must buy fresh, a couple of hours before a meal since its

. . . .

MARCEL HAUPOIS PAUSES MOMEN-
TARILY IN HIS KITCHEN DURING A
NORMALLY HECTIC MORNING.

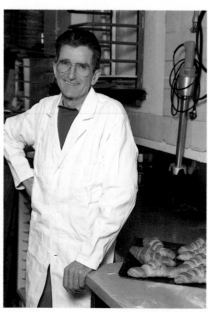

shelflife is very short. We have customers who buy one baguette to have with their lunch and then return at the end of the day to buy another to accompany their dinner."

In addition to his classic breads and *pâtisseries,* such as fruit tarts, éclairs, and meringues, Monsieur Haupois offers his special *gougères,* big round Gruyère cheese puffs made from lighter-than-air *choux* pastry, a perfect accompaniment to a light soup-and-salad dinner or wonderful served with aperitifs. Other attractions within this seventeenth-century edifice, part of an early "urban development project" sanctioned by Louis XIII, are a handful of original *pâtisseries* that Monsieur Haupois developed and named for the *île.* Among them are the little round Saint-Louis, dense and chocolatey, and the unique Croquets Bourbonnais, crisp, flat, paper-thin nougatine cookies named for the nearby quai de Bourbon and superb served with rich vanilla or coffee ice cream. No one wandering the little *rues* and broad *quais* of this unusual enclave should miss stopping in to the Boulangerie Haupois for a true taste of the *île.*

❀

Croquets Bourbonnais

. . . .

[CRUNCHY ALMOND
HAZELNUT WAFERS]

. . . .

Many of Monsieur Haupois's customers buy these hard and very crunchy nut cookies to accompany vanilla or coffee ice cream.

¼ POUND/125 G WHOLE
HAZELNUTS

¼ POUND/125 G WHOLE ALMONDS

2 ¼ CUPS/625 G DARK BROWN
SUGAR

2 CUPS PLUS 2 TABLESPOONS/
300 G ALL-PURPOSE UNBLEACHED
FLOUR, SIFTED

¾ CUP/175 ML EGG WHITES
(4 OR 5 EGGS)

1 TABLESPOON VANILLA EXTRACT

HAUPOIS'S WINDOW FEATURES CROQUETS BOURBONNAIS, CRUNCHY NUT WAFERS THAT ARE PERFECT WITH ICE CREAM.

Preheat oven to 375°F./190°C. Grind the hazelnuts and almonds together in a food processor until finely chopped. In a large bowl, combine the nuts, sugar, flour, egg whites and vanilla, and mix well with an electric mixer until well blended. (The cohesiveness of the dough depends entirely on the egg white; since the viscous quality of egg white in each egg is quite variable—sometimes very liquid, sometimes gelatinous—the dough may at first be too dry or too sticky.) If the dough does not come together and remains crumbly, add another egg white; if the dough is too sticky, add more flour, a tablespoon or two at a time, until dough is firm. It may be easier at this point to mix the dough with a wooden spoon or even your hands, adding flour and kneading it in until dough no longer sticks to your fingers.

On a well-floured work surface, with a well-floured rolling pin, roll out half the dough with brisk, one-way strokes into a rectangle about 10 x 14 inches/25 x 35 cm and ⅛ inch/3 mm thick. (Monsieur Haupois rolls his dough paper-thin, which is ideal, but hard to do.) Trim

....

PAINS AUX RAISINS ARE POPULAR IN PARIS FOR SUNDAY BREAKFAST.

all sides into straight edges, then cut the dough into rectangles about 3 x 4 inches/7 x 10 cm. With a wide metal spatula, carefully lift and transfer each piece onto a well-greased baking sheet. Brush pieces with the beaten egg so that tops are evenly covered. Repeat with other half of the dough. Bake in one or two batches for about 12 to 15 minutes, until edges are brown. Remove to a wire rack and let cool completely. The wafers can be stored in an airtight container for up to four days.

MAKES ABOUT 12 LARGE WAFERS

❋

Pains au Raisins

....

[RAISIN BUN SWIRLS]

....

These delicious raisin buns, another classic French breakfast treat, are, like the croissant and the brioche, a legacy of the nineteenth-century Viennese bakers of Paris.

¼ CUP/60 ML DARK RUM

½ CUP/40 G SEEDLESS RAISINS

1 RECIPE BRIOCHE DOUGH (PAGE 45), PREPARED AND CHILLED OVERNIGHT IN THE REFRIGERATOR

1 RECIPE CRÈME PÂTISSIÈRE (PAGE 146)

3 TABLESPOONS GRANULATED SUGAR MIXED WITH 1 TEASPOON CINNAMON (OPTIONAL)

1 LARGE EGG, BEATEN, FOR GLAZE

½ CUP/70 G CONFECTIONERS' SUGAR

In a small bowl, combine the rum and the raisins. Cover with plastic wrap and let soak several hours or, even better, overnight. Drain in a strainer and set aside the excess rum. On a floured work surface, roll out the brioche dough into a 14-inch/35-cm square, about ⅛ inch/⅓ cm thick. Trim the sides to make a precise square. Spread the *crème pâtissière* over the dough with a spatula or a palette knife. Scatter the raisins evenly over the *crème*, then sprinkle

the sugar-and-cinnamon mixture over the raisins. Using a large palette knife to carefully lift up one side of the dough from the surface, roll the sheet like a jelly roll into a long slim cylinder, or a *boudin*—a sausage—as the French say. Slice the roll into pieces just under 1 inch/2½ cm-wide and set flat 2 inches/5 cm apart on a baking sheet moistened with a damp pastry brush. Slightly flatten each piece with the palm of your hand, then brush the tops with the beaten egg. Let rise, uncovered, for about 1 hour in a draft-free place, until the pieces double in volume. Preheat the oven to 425°F./220°C.

Brush the pieces with another coat of beaten egg, then set on the center rack of the oven. Bake about 15 minutes, until golden brown. Remove from the oven and remove with a spatula to cool on a wire rack. *Do not shut off the oven.* Mix 1 tablespoon of the reserved rum with the confectioners' sugar and stir into a thin, smooth paste. When the *pains aux raisins* have cooled, brush the tops with the sugar mix, using a pastry brush. Arrange the pastries again on the baking sheet and return to the oven for 1 to 2 minutes, just until the sugar melts and becomes transparent. Remove from the baking sheet immediately. Serve warm or at room temperature.

MAKES ABOUT 12 PIECES

❋

Croissants

....

Croissants arrived in Paris with the influx of Viennese bakers in the mid-nineteenth century. The origin of the croissant is generally attributed to a group of seventeenth-century bakers in Vienna, who were instrumental in repelling an invasion of Turks who attacked the Austrian capital in 1683. The bakers, who were of course awake and working in the middle of the night, heard the enemy forces

HAUPOIS CROISSANTS STAR AT A BREAKFAST TABLE SET WITH ANTIQUE TABLEWARE FROM ISABELLE PILATE.

THE BURNISHED OAK FACADE OF THE BOULANGERIE HAUPOIS DISTINGUISHES
THE BAKERY FROM ITS STONE-FACED NEIGHBORS.

. . . .

burrowing a tunnel under the city's ramparts and sounded the alert. To celebrate the defeat of the Turks, they created a pastry using the crescent from the Turkish flag as a motif.

Croissants are a pastry in the *pâte levée*—leavened pastry dough—category, as are the brioche and the *kugelhopf*, which all take time and care to produce. It is best to begin preparations the night before you intend to serve them. Croissants are best prepared in a cool kitchen so that the temperamental buttery croissant dough remains firm but pliant.

2 TABLESPOONS PLUS
1 TEASPOON (ABOUT 2 ½
PACKAGES) DRY YEAST

⅓ CUP/70 ML WATER, AT ROOM
TEMPERATURE

4 CUPS/568 G CAKE FLOUR

¼ CUP/50 G SUGAR

1 TABLESPOON SALT

1 CUP/250 ML MILK, AT ROOM
TEMPERATURE

1 CUP (2 STICKS)/
250 G UNSALTED BUTTER,
COOL BUT JUST MALLEABLE

1 LARGE EGG, BEATEN

In a small bowl, combine the yeast with the water, stirring to dissolve. Let stand 5 minutes. In a large bowl, combine the flour, sugar, salt, milk, and the yeast mixture, stirring with a wooden spoon, then mixing with your hands to blend or in an electric mixer with a dough hook attachment. When the dough can form a ball, turn it out onto a floured work surface, kneading gently for 5 minutes, pushing the dough flat against the surface and gathering it together several times. Knead just until the dough is smooth and a bit firm but still soft in texture. The less kneading the better with croissant dough, since too much kneading toughens the dough. Form the dough into a ball, place in the center of a greased bowl, cover with plastic wrap, and let rise 1 hour at room temperature, then transfer to the refrigerator and let rise for another ½ hour. On a lightly floured surface, roll out the dough into a rectangle approximately 9 x 15 inches/23 x 38 cm and ⅜ inch/1 cm thick. Let the dough rest for 5 minutes.

Check the butter to make sure it is precisely the right temperature and texture—not hard and cold so that it will break through the dough, not warm and greasy so that it will smear, but cool and just malleable. Monsieur Haupois says that the butter should have almost the same consistency as the dough. If the butter is hard, work it with the heel of your hand or a dough scraper against the work surface to soften slightly, or work it between 2 sheets of wax paper. If it is too warm and soft, chill it in the refrigerator for several minutes. Flatten the butter so that it forms a 5 x 7-inch/12 x 8-cm rectangle ½ inch/1 cm thick.

Place the butter on the bottom third of the dough rectangle. Fold the top third down over the center of the dough. Fold the bottom third up over the top third, as though you were folding a business letter. Press the sides and the center seam closed with your hands to seal. On a floured surface, with a floured rolling pin, roll out the dough lengthwise into a rectangle about 3 times its original size; it should be about ¾ inch/2 cm thick and 16 inches/40 cm long. Fold it in thirds again, letter style. Set on a platter and chill, uncovered, in the refrigerator for 10 minutes.

On a floured surface, roll out the dough again lengthwise to a rectangle 3 times its original length. Fold it in thirds, letter style. Chill for 10 minutes. Roll out into a rectangle one more time, and again fold in thirds. Each folding and rolling process is called a "turn," and the dough has now undergone a classic series of 4 turns. Dust the dough with flour, wrap in plastic wrap or wax paper and chill in the refrigerator for at least 2 hours, or up to a maximum of 24 hours, tightly wrapped in plastic to seal in moisture over the long rest.

On a floured surface, roll out the dough into a long, flat rectangle, about 12 x 30 inches/30 x 76 cm and ¼ inch/½ cm thick. Using a yardstick and a pastry cutter or sharp chef's knife, cut the rectangle in half lengthwise, then trim all sides so that the edges are straight and true. Using a sharp chef's knife, cut the dough into precise triangles, 6 inches/15 cm from tip to base and about 5 inches/13 cm across the base. The triangles will alternate base and tip along the length of the dough, that is, the first triangle will be cut with the base of the triangle on the bottom, tip of the triangle on the top, then the next will be cut base of the triangle at the top, tip of the triangle on the bottom. When all the triangles are cut, roll them into crescents; beginning at the base and using the fingertips of both hands, gently roll the dough toward the tip until completely rolled. Repeat with each triangle.

Dampen 1 or 2 sturdy baking sheets with a moist pastry brush. Transfer the croissants to the baking sheet about 2 inches/5 cm apart, placing them so that the tip of the triangle is tucked under the body of the croissant. Gently bend the ends of the croissant toward the center to form the crescent shape, then press the ends ever so gently into the baking sheet to anchor them, but without thinning the dough. Brush the croissants lightly with the beaten egg, then set aside to rise, uncovered, at room temperature for about 2 hours. Twenty minutes before baking, preheat the oven to 425°F./220°C.

Brush the croissants with another coat of beaten egg. Set the baking sheets in the center of the oven, reduce the temperature to 400°F./200°C., and bake 15 to 20 minutes, until they are a burnished golden brown. Cool on a rack and serve warm or at room temperature. (If you use 2 baking sheets but can only bake 1 sheet at a time, refrigerate the second batch, uncovered, as the first batch bakes.)

MAKES 14 TO 16 CROISSANTS

- - - - - - - - - - - -

THE OVERSIZED HAUPOIS GOUGÈRES, GRUYÈRE CHEESE PUFFS, ARE IRRE-
SISTIBLE SERVED AT LUNCH, AS A SNACK, OR WITH COCKTAILS.

Gougères

- - - - - - - - - - - -

[GIANT GRUYÈRE CHEESE
PUFFS]

- - - - - - - - - - - -

These huge, round cheese puffs made with *pâte à choux*, or cream puff dough, are rich but lighter than air. Served in a large, rustic basket, they are the first things to disappear from a buffet table.

6 TABLESPOONS/90 G UNSALTED
BUTTER, CUT INTO BITS

1 CUP/250 ML WATER

PINCH OF SALT

PINCH OF WHITE PEPPER

1½ CUPS/200 G ALL-PURPOSE
UNBLEACHED FLOUR, SIFTED

6 LARGE EGGS

2 CUPS/180 G COARSELY SHRED-
DED GRUYÈRE CHEESE

Preheat the oven to 400°F./200°C. In a small saucepan, combine the butter, water, and salt. Bring to a boil over high heat; then remove from the heat and stir in the pepper and the flour with a wooden spoon. Reduce the heat to medium. Return to the heat and stir vigorously with a wooden spoon until the mixture becomes very thick and begins to film the bottom of the saucepan, about 1 minute. Remove from the heat. Add the eggs to the mixture one by one, stirring vigorously with a wooden spoon. The dough should have the consistency of a thick mayonnaise. Stir in 1½ cups/120 g of the cheese.

On a buttered and floured baking sheet or one lined with parchment paper, drop heaping tablespoonfuls of dough, spacing them at least 2 inches/5 cm apart. Sprinkle the puffs with the remaining ½ cup/120 g of Gruyère. Bake about 25 minutes, until the puffs swell to almost triple in size and become golden. Cool on a wire rack and serve warm.

MAKES 12 TO 14 LARGE PUFFS

AMONG THE MANY POPULAR BREADS CHEZ HAUPOIS IS LA GALETTE, THE
FLATTENED BAGUETTE, IN THE CENTER OF THE BASKET, DESIGNED FOR
THOSE WHO LOVE THE CRUST.

. . . .

La Galette (Baguette Aplati)

. . . .

["PANCAKE" OR "FLATTENED"
BAGUETTE]

. . . .

This popular bread, created for those
who love a lot of crust and little
crumb, can be formed from classic
baguette dough (page 126), from the
Pain de Campagne recipe (page 107),
or from the recipe below. The
doughs are simply pressed flat as a
pancake before the final rising.

STARTER

1 TABLESPOON YEAST

½ CUP/125 ML WATER, AT ROOM
TEMPERATURE

1 CUP/125 G HARD WHEAT OR
UNBLEACHED ALL-PURPOSE
FLOUR

. . . .

DOUGH

3 CUPS/375 G HARD WHEAT OR
UNBLEACHED ALL-PURPOSE
FLOUR

1 CUP/250 ML WATER, AT ROOM
TEMPERATURE

2 TEASPOONS SALT

CORNMEAL, FOR DUSTING

STARTER: In a small bowl, combine
the yeast and water, stirring well to
dissolve the yeast. Set aside for 5
minutes. In a large bowl, combine
the flour with the yeast mixture and
stir vigorously with a wooden spoon
to mix well. With your hands or in
the bowl of an electric mixer
equipped with a dough hook, knead
the starter for about 8 to 10 minutes,
until it is smooth and supple. If
working by hand, transfer the dough
to a lightly floured surface to knead.
Form the dough into a ball and set
into a clean, greased bowl. Cover
with a cloth and set aside to rise in a

draft-free place for 2 hours, or until
doubled in size.

DOUGH: Add the flour, water, and
salt to the starter and knead in the
bowl to blend the ingredients. If
using a dough hook, put the starter
in the bowl of an electric mixer, add
the flour, water, and salt, and mix
until blended. Then knead until the
dough is supple and elastic. If working by hand, turn the dough onto a
lightly floured work surface and continue kneading until the dough is
supple and elastic, about 10 to 15
minutes. If the dough is too sticky,
add a tablespoon or two of flour; if
the dough is too dense and hard to
work, add a tablespoon or two of
room-temperature water. Form the
dough into a ball, return to a greased
bowl, cover with a cloth, and let rise
about 45 minutes. Divide the dough
into 2 equal portions.

On a floured work surface, roll out
each piece of dough round and flat,
about 10 inches/25 cm in diameter
and ½ inch/1 cm thick. Transfer the
dough rounds to a baking sheet dusted with cornmeal. Cover the 2
rounds with a cloth and let rise about
1½ hours. (This bread is also delicious formed into a traditional long
baguette, loaf, with a tasty golden
crumb that is not very apparent in a
flattened, all-crust loaf. With this
recipe you could make 1 flattened
baguette and 1 long loaf.)

Preheat the oven to 450°F./
230°C. Using a razor or the tip of a
very sharp knife, slash the top of the
loaf with shallow crosshatchings.
Place a baking pan of hot water on
the floor of the oven. Bake the bread
on the center rack for 20 minutes.
Remove the pan of water. Continue
baking for 10 minutes. Then turn
the temperature down to 400°F./
200°C. and bake for another 7 to 10
minutes, until the loaf is golden
brown. Cool the loaves on a wire
rack.

MAKES 2 FLAT LOAVES,
EACH ABOUT 10 INCHES/
25 CM IN DIAMETER

Pain de Campagne

···········

[HEARTY COUNTRY LOAF]

···········

This method of bread making—*sur poolish*—involves making a starter with about one-third of the flour and two-thirds of the water from the total ingredients, which ferments from 1½ to 2 hours. The process originated in the nineteenth century in Paris, introduced by the newly installed Viennese bakers. Bread made *sur poolish,* which has come back in vogue among several top bakers after years of obscurity, benefits from three fermentations rather than the standard two, and has a more pronounced yeasty flavor and slightly more acidity than classic white bread.

POOLISH

1¼ CUPS/177 G HARD WHEAT OR UNBLEACHED ALL-PURPOSE FLOUR

1 TABLESPOON DRY YEAST

1 CUP PLUS 2 TABLESPOONS / 280 ML WATER, AT ROOM TEMPERATURE

···········

DOUGH

1 TABLESPOON DRY YEAST

½ CUP/125 ML WATER, AT ROOM TEMPERATURE

1¼ CUPS/177 G HARD WHEAT OR UNBLEACHED ALL-PURPOSE FLOUR

1¼ CUPS/177 G WHOLE WHEAT FLOUR

1 TABLESPOON SEA SALT

UNBLEACHED ALL-PURPOSE FLOUR, FOR SPRINKLING

POOLISH: In a medium bowl, combine all of the ingredients, stirring well with a whisk until a thin, smooth batter forms. Set aside, uncovered, for 2 hours in a draft-free place.

DOUGH: In a small bowl, combine the yeast and water, stirring well to dissolve the yeast. Set aside 5 minutes. In a large bowl, combine the flours, salt, yeast mixture, and the *poolish* and mix well. When all ingredients are blended and a ball of dough is formed, turn it out onto a floured work surface and knead the dough vigorously, using the heels of your hands frequently, for 10 to 12 minutes, until the dough is supple and elastic. If the dough is too sticky, sprinkle in a bit of flour; if the dough is too dense and unpliable, sprinkle in a few drops of room-temperature water. Form the dough into a ball, place in a lightly greased bowl, cover with a cloth, and let rise for 2 hours.

On a floured work surface, punch down the dough vigorously, releasing all the accumulated gases, kneading the dough 3 to 5 minutes. Form the dough into a ball. With 3 fingers pressed lightly on top of the ball of dough and the other hand holding the dough steady at the side, make a 45-degree turn with your top hand, making a swirl in the surface of the dough. Place your hand again in the center of the dough and repeat the turn. Do twice more. These turns give the interior of the bread better texture. Form the dough again into a smooth ball and place on a baking sheet lightly sprinkled with flour or cornmeal, pressing down gently so that a flat bottom forms. Cover with a cloth and let rise 1 to 1½ hours in a draft-free place until the dough doubles in volume. Preheat the oven to 425°F./220°C. Sprinkle the top of the bread with a bit of flour. With a razor, slit the top of the bread in a crosshatch, tictacktoe design, but with 3 lines in each direction. Place a baking pan of hot water on the floor of the oven. This helps approximate the moist environment of the French baker's oven. Bake the bread on the bottom rack for 30 minutes. Reduce the temperature to 400°F./ 200°C. and bake another 15 to 20 minutes, until the top of the bread is deep golden brown.

MAKES 1 ROUND 10-INCH/ 25-CM LOAF

···········

OUTSIDE THE BOULANGERIE HAUPOIS, THE RUE DES DEUX PONTS LEADS TO THE PONT MARIE AND OVER THE SEINE TO THE RIGHT BANK.

Les Jeunes Artisans
Extraordinaires

JEAN-LUC POUJAURAN

MOULIN DE LA VIERGE

GÉRARD MULOT

AU PÉCHÉ MIGNON

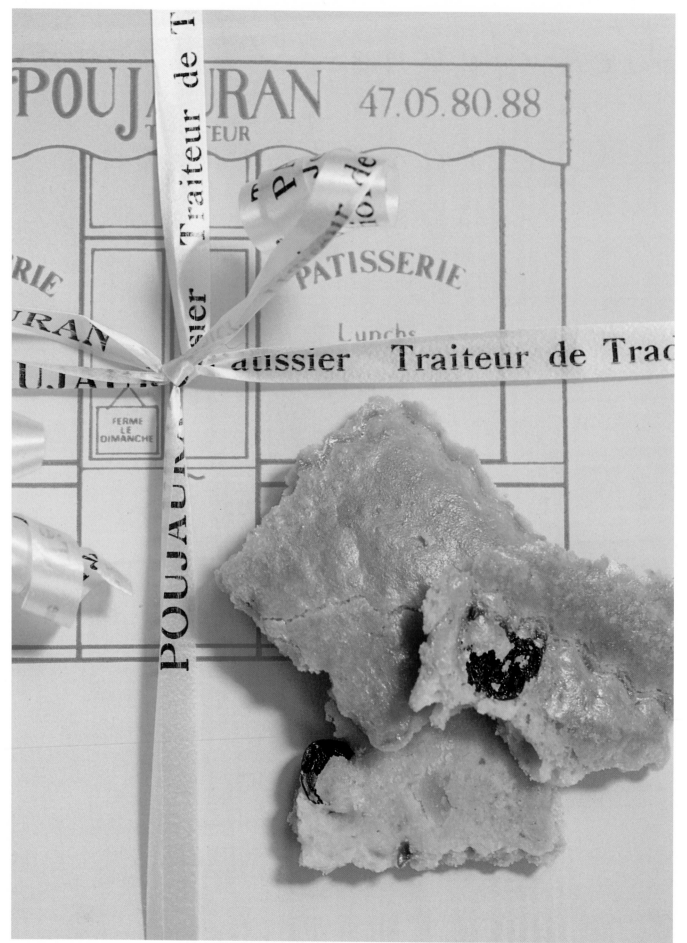

JEAN-LUC POUJAURAN'S FLAKY SABLÉS À L'ORANGE ET RAISINS ARE A HOUSE SPECIALTY.

Sablés à l'Orange et Raisins

Pain au Maïs · Gâteau Basque

Pâte Feuilletée au Jambon et Fromage

Feuilletage

Tarte aux Pommes Rissolées

The rue Jean-Nicot is a tiny, nondescript street in the shadow of the Eiffel Tower. One blink as you're driving along the busy rue St. Dominique and you've missed it. Yet it is here, amidst the uninspired low-rise apartments, a couple of dim *café-tabacs,* and a notions shop, that the world-class *boulangerie-pâtisserie* of Jean-Luc Poujauran prepares some of the best breads, croissants, and rustic *pâtisseries* that Paris has to offer. The minuscule shop with its bright pink facade the color of raspberry mousse attracts bread lovers from all over the Left Bank and beyond; the little blue Poujauran delivery truck, looking like it jumped from the pages of a children's storybook, disseminates his wares even farther afield—to hotels like the Crillon, to more than sixty restaurants in Paris and the suburbs, and to such discriminating croissant lovers as François Mitterrand, the president of France.

The winsome little Poujauran *boulangerie,* with its original turn-of-the-century decor and intimate ambience, tugs at the heartstrings, as does the charismatic Jean-Luc. With his thick, shaggy hair, intense, deep-set blue eyes, and his perpetual four-day growth of beard, this is a baker who might easily have forged a second career in the films of Louis Malle. When asked what it takes to be a great baker, he answers with an ironic smile, *"Il faut être grand, fort, et bête,"* repeating the rather cruel old saw about the qualifications for a baker's apprentice—"You must be big, strong, and stupid." In Jean-Luc's case,

POUJAURAN'S OLD-FASHIONED BLUE DELIVERY TRUCK IS EQUIPPED WITH A
WICKER ROOF RACK TO DISPERSE HIS BREADS THROUGHOUT PARIS.

himself. As it is, he is up before dawn and works well into the late evening.

There are some hard-liners in the Paris baking trade who believe that no one can be both a good *pâtissier* and a good *boulanger*. For them it is an either-or proposition. But in these days when almost all *boulangers* make pastries and most *pâtissiers* offer some sort of bread, the line between the two vocations becomes blurred. When Jean-Luc, born to and trained by a baker, then trained as a *pâtissier*, and visibly succeeding enormously at both undertakings, is asked which he truly is in his heart, he is hard-pressed to answer. But after watching him at work and listening to him talk at length about the related métiers, it is hard not to draw your own conclusion. "The process of making *pâtisserie* is a little more *équilibré*, a little more stable and sure, than bread making," he says. "*Pâtisserie* is more like chemistry, like a controlled chemical formula—you combine certain ingredients a certain way, heat them at an exact temperature for a set length of time,

1

A SIGN NOTES THAT ALL PASTRIES
ARE MADE WITH PURE BUTTER.

the apparent qualifications are "savvy, ambitious, demanding, years of top-level, on-the-job training, an ineffable feel for the flour, and a deep respect for the traditions of French *boulange*, the baker's trade." Jean-Luc is a proud native of the Landes region deep in France's southwest, and the son of a top provincial baker. He started working early on at his father's side, after school and on weekends. "I was seven or eight," remembers Jean-Luc, "and right away I loved the work. By the time I was fourteen I had moved to Paris and was working in a bakery." He went on to add several of the best *pâtisseries* to his résumé, among them La Petite Marquise and Ladurée, before scraping together the resources—including funds from faithful customers—to open his own shop in 1977 on Jean-Nicot where it flourishes today.

His personal appeal notwithstanding, it is the fine and distinctive breads and *pâtisseries* that draw the customers chez Poujauran—his dense, tangy *pain de campagne;* the chewy, flavorful *baguette;* the *Pain de Seigle aux Raisins,* an intense dark

rye with raisins; his *Pain au Maïs,* a delicious corn bread; his amber-toned *Tarte aux Pommes Rissolées,* a luscious tart of sautéed apples and almond cream; a classic, regional *Gâteau Basque,* richly flavored with almond; the *Tartes aux Pignons,* little pine nut tarts; and the *Sablés à l'Orange et Raisins,* the light, buttery cookies flavored with orange zest made from his father's recipe. All his products are created from organic, stone-ground flours specially milled for him at an old mill in Précy-sur-Marne, north of Paris. The ground-floor *laboratoire,* where the pastries are made behind the shop, and the below-stairs *fournil,* where the breads are produced, function twenty-four hours a day, with his eighteen employees working shifts around the clock. With the demands of his bakery, the size of which belies the vast scope of his business, and increasing daily requests from around the world for his consulting services from commercial bakers who want to improve the quality of their breads or entrepreneurs who want to establish bakeshop boutiques, Jean-Luc could easily work a twenty-four-hour day

OUTSIDE OF HIS SHOP ON THE RUE JEAN-NICOT, JEAN-LUC POUJAURAN
ENJOYS THE FRUITS OF HIS LABOR.

and you have the expected result. Bread is a more capricious composition that in subtle ways is always different. Bread is never the same twice because of so many variables. The flour is never exactly the same; the humidity of the *fournil* constantly varies; the temperature of the oven is never exactly the same; and the mood and temperament of the man making the bread is never the same, one day to the next. Like a good wine or cheese, bread responds to everything in its environment." It is evident that beneath this man's crisp white *pâtissier's* jacket beats the heart of a born *boulanger*.

❋

Sablés à l'Orange et Raisins

....

[ORANGE AND RAISIN COOKIES]

....

1/2 CUP (1 STICK) PLUS 2 TABLESPOONS/150 G UNSALTED BUTTER, SOFTENED

1/3 CUP/60 G SUGAR

1 LARGE EGG

1 LARGE EGG YOLK

2 TABLESPOONS GROUND ALMONDS

1 2/3 CUPS/260 G ALL-PURPOSE FLOUR

1 TEASPOON BAKING POWDER

1/2 CUP/70 G CURRANTS OR RAISINS

1/4 CUP/60 G CHOPPED CANDIED ORANGE PEEL (OR GRATED ZEST OF 1 ORANGE)

1 LARGE EGG BEATEN WITH 1 TEASPOON WATER, FOR GLAZE

In a large bowl with an electric mixer, cream the butter with the sugar until light. Add the egg, egg yolk, and almonds in turn, mixing after each addition until well blended. Sift the flour with the baking powder and add to the butter mixture, mixing just until partially incorporated. Add the currants and orange peel and finish mixing the dough with a large rubber spatula just until blended. Be careful not to overmix. Wrap the dough in plastic and refrigerate for at least 1 hour.

Preheat the oven to 350°F./175°C. Lightly butter 2 baking sheets. Roll out the dough on a lightly floured surface about 1/8 inch/1/3 cm thick. Cut out the cookies with a round cookie cutter, or any other shapes you like, and place the cookies on the prepared sheets. Brush the cookies lightly with the egg wash. Bake until light golden, about 13 minutes. Watch carefully so the cookies do not overbake.

Cool the pan briefly on a wire rack, then carefully transfer the cookies from the pan to the rack with a spatula. Cool completely. These cookies keep well, stored in an airtight container, up to 2 weeks.

MAKES ABOUT 3 DOZEN COOKIES

❋

Pain au Maïs

....

[CORN BREAD]

....

In many parts of France, corn has long been considered suitable only for animal feed. But in the Pays Basque, in southwestern France, cornmeal has always been used for cooking, particularly in this tasty version of corn bread that combines both cornmeal and whole corn kernels.

....

THE RECIPE FOR JEAN-LUC'S SABLÉS À L'ORANGE ET RAISINS COOKIES COMES FROM HIS BAKER FATHER.

POUJAURAN'S PAIN AU MAÏS IS
THE IDEAL FOIL TO SAUCISSON SEC,
DRIED SAUSAGE, OR FOIE GRAS.

. . . .

1 ¼ CUPS LUKEWARM WATER

4 ½ TEASPOONS (1 ½ ENVELOPES)
DRY YEAST

1 EGG, LIGHTLY BEATEN

3 ¾ CUPS/475 G ALL-PURPOSE
OR BREAD FLOUR

1 CUP/150 G CORNMEAL

4 TABLESPOONS/50 G UNSALTED
BUTTER, SOFTENED

1 TABLESPOON SALT

⅔ CUP/125 G CORN KERNELS,
FRESH, CANNED AND DRAINED,
OR THAWED FROZEN

Combine the lukewarm water and yeast in a small bowl; let stand for 5 minutes. Stir in the egg.

Place the flour and cornmeal in the bowl of an electric mixer fitted with a dough hook or in a large mixing bowl, and mix until blended. Make a well in the center of the flour mixture and pour in the yeast mixture. Begin to mix until the dough comes together, either by machine or, if by hand, gradually incorporate the ingredients together with your hand, then blend with your fingers as it comes together. Add the butter and salt and knead the dough with the dough hook or by hand on a lightly floured surface until smooth and elastic, 8 to 10 minutes. Knead

in the corn kernels until they are evenly distributed.

Place the dough in a lightly buttered bowl, turning to coat with butter. Cover the bowl with a towel and let the dough rise in a draft-free place until doubled in volume, about 1 hour.

Butter two 8 x 4-inch/20 x 10-cm loaf pans. Punch down the dough and divide it in 2 equal pieces. On a countertop or cutting board covered with wax paper, pat each piece into a rectangle about 8 inches/20 cm wide and ¾ inch/2 cm thick. Beginning with a short end, roll each piece of dough into a loaf shape and place it seam side down into a pan. Cover the pans with the towel and let the dough rise until it comes nearly to the rim of the pan, about 1 hour.

Preheat the oven to 400°F./200°C. Place a shallow pan of hot water on the lower rack to create steam. With a razor blade or paring knife, quickly cut 2 crosswise lines in the surface of each loaf without deflating it.

Bake on a rack in the middle of the oven until golden brown, about 1 hour. If the loaves begin to get too brown before they have baked through, lay a sheet of aluminum foil lightly on the surface of the breads. Invert the loaves onto a wire rack and allow them to cool completely before slicing.

MAKES 2 LOAVES

✳

Gâteau Basque ✓

. . . .

This delightfully rich almond cake is a traditional sweet in the Pays Basque region of southwestern France, which is the area just north of the Spanish border.

PÂTE (DOUGH)

½ CUP (1 STICK)/125 G UNSALT-
ED BUTTER, SOFTENED

½ CUP/100 G SUGAR

2 LARGE EGGS

GRATED ZEST OF 1 SMALL LEMON

1 TEASPOON VANILLA EXTRACT

2 CUPS LESS 2 TABLESPOONS/
500 G ALL-PURPOSE FLOUR

1 ½ TEASPOONS BAKING POWDER

. . . .

CRÈME D'AMANDES (ALMOND CREAM)

⅓ CUP PLUS 1 TABLESPOON/
95 G SUGAR

1 ⅓ CUPS/125 G SLICED OR
COARSE-CHOPPED ALMONDS

½ CUP (1 STICK)/125 G
UNSALTED BUTTER, SOFTENED

1 LARGE EGG

1 LARGE EGG YOLK

2 TABLESPOONS RUM

1 ½ TEASPOONS VANILLA EXTRACT

¼ TEASPOON LEMON EXTRACT

. . . .

GLAZE

1 BEATEN EGG

PÂTE (DOUGH): With an electric mixer, cream the butter and sugar until light, then add the eggs and beat until smooth. Add the lemon zest and vanilla. Stir together the flour and baking powder and add to the butter mixture, mixing just until blended. Don't overmix. Wrap in plastic and refrigerate for at least 1 hour.

. . . .

FILLED WITH ALMOND CREAM, THE
GÂTEAU BASQUE IS A DELICIOUS
SPECIALTY FROM FRANCE'S BASQUE
COUNTRY IN THE DEEP SOUTHWEST.

CRÈME D'AMANDES (ALMOND CREAM): Grind the sugar and almonds in a food processor until powdery. Add all the remaining ingredients and process until smooth.

ASSEMBLY: Preheat the oven to 375°F./190°C. Butter a 9-inch/23-cm round cake pan. Cut off about one-third of the dough and return it, wrapped, to the refrigerator. This dough is somewhat delicate to handle and it should be kept as cold as possible, though malleable enough to roll. Roll out the larger piece of dough on a lightly floured sheet of wax paper to 11 inches/28 cm diameter, about ⅛ inch/⅓ cm thick; invert it into the pan without stretching and peel off the paper. Brush a 1-inch/2½-cm strip around the edge of the dough with the beaten egg.

Scrape the almond cream into the dough and spread evenly to cover the bottom and sides. Roll the remaining piece of refrigerated dough on a floured sheet of wax paper into a neat 9-inch/23-cm round, trimming it to just fit the top of the pan. Invert

....

ANTIQUE BAKER'S RACKS ARE PART OF THE TURN-OF-THE-CENTURY DECOR THAT GIVES JEAN-LUC'S BAKERY SO MUCH CHARM.

the round of dough onto the cream and gently peel off and discard the paper. Gently press the edges of the pastry around the rim of the pan to seal. Carefully trim off the excess dough from the sides. Brush the surface with the egg wash. With a fork, make a diagonal crisscross pattern of lines in the dough.

Bake for about 40 minutes, or until the pastry is golden brown. Cool the cake in the pan on a wire rack for 10 or 15 minutes. Carefully invert the cake, remove the pan, then turn right-side up again. Serve at room temperature.

MAKES 6 TO 8 SERVINGS

....

VARIATION: TARTES AUX PIGNONS
(PINE NUT TARTS)

1 RECIPE GÂTEAU BASQUE DOUGH
(ABOVE)

1 RECIPE CRÈME D'AMANDES
(ABOVE)

¾ CUP/100 G PINE NUTS,
OR AS NEEDED

Preheat the oven to 375°F./190°C. Butter eight 4- to 4½-inch/10- to 11-cm or twelve 3-inch/8-cm tartlet molds, or sixteen 2½-inch/6-cm muffin tins. Roll out the dough on a lightly floured sheet of wax paper to about ⅛ inch/⅓ cm thick. Cut out rounds of dough about 1 inch larger than the diameter of the molds. Fit the rounds of dough into the molds without stretching and trim the edges.

With a tablespoon or a pastry bag with a plain tip, divide the almond cream among the pastry shells, filling them about half full. Sprinkle the surface of each tart with pine nuts.

Bake until the tarts are golden, 20 to 25 minutes for tartlets, about 17 minutes in a muffin pan. The timing will vary based on the size of the molds, so watch carefully. Cool the tarts in their pans on a wire rack for about 10 minutes. Carefully unmold and cool to room temperature.

MAKES 6 TO 8 SERVINGS

THE PÂTE FEUILLETÉE AU JAMBON ET FROMAGE TEMPTS DAILY FROM THE BAKERY WINDOW.

....

Pâte Feuilletée au Jambon et Fromage

....

[PUFF PASTRY PIE WITH HAM AND GRUYÈRE

....

This makes a hearty first course, or a wonderful light lunch or supper accompanied by a crisp green salad.

1 RECIPE PUFF PASTRY DOUGH
(PAGE 116)

....

BÉCHAMEL WITH GRUYÈRE
FILLING

1 CUP/125 ML MILK

8 OUNCES/250 G GRATED
GRUYÈRE CHEESE

2 LARGE EGGS, LIGHTLY BEATEN

½ CUP/125 ML CRÈME FRAÎCHE
OR HEAVY CREAM

½ CUP/100 G ALL-PURPOSE
FLOUR

SALT AND FRESHLY GROUND
PEPPER

PINCH OF NUTMEG

¼ POUND/125 G BAKED HAM
IN 2 TO 4 THIN SLICES

....

GLAZE

1 LARGE EGG, LIGHTLY BEATEN
WITH 1 TABLESPOON WATER

Preheat the oven to 400°F./200°C. Divide the dough in half. Roll out each half on a lightly floured surface or between 2 sheets of lightly floured wax paper to a thickness of ⅛ inch/⅓ cm. Turn a 10-inch/25-cm tart pan or slope-sided ovenproof skillet upside down and press into the dough. Cut around the perimeter to obtain a neat circle of dough. Brush the bottom and sides of the baking pan with a pastry brush dampened with cold water. Press 1 circle of pastry crust into the bottom and slightly up the sides of the tart pan or skillet. Cut out the remaining circle of dough. Refrigerate all pastry.

BÉCHAMEL WITH GRUYERE FILL-ING: In a large heavy saucepan, combine the milk and cheese. Bring to a boil over medium heat, stirring constantly until the cheese has melted completely. Remove from the heat and set aside.

In a heavy medium saucepan, combine the eggs with the crème fraîche. Over medium heat, stir to blend. Add the flour, salt and pepper, and nutmeg, stirring constantly to keep the bottom from burning. Reduce the heat to low and simmer for 5 minutes. Do not allow the mixture to boil. Remove from the heat and pour into the cheese mixture, mixing well with a wooden spoon to blend. Let cool.

Spread one-half of the béchamel mixture over the bottom of the pastry shell, leaving a 1-inch/2½-cm border up the sides uncovered. Lay the ham slices evenly over the béchamel mixture. Spread the remaining béchamel mixture over the ham. Lay the other circle of dough over the ham and cheese filling. Seal the pastry crust by pinching together the 2 halves (or close using a butter knife and pressing the dough all around into a vertical "ridge" pattern) *inside* the pan so that the seam is about ½ inch/1 cm

below the top of the pan. (The pastry does not meet at the top of the pan as in a standard pie or covered tart.) Brush the top of the pie with egg glaze, then score it in a crosshatch pattern and make a small, ½-inch/1-cm hole in the center of the top crust—a *chéminée*, as Jean-Luc says—to let the steam out as it bakes. Bake in the center of the oven for 15 minutes. Reduce the heat to 350°F./175°C. and continue baking about another 30 minutes, until the crust is deep golden brown. Cool slightly on a wire rack before serving.

MAKES 6 TO 8 SERVINGS

⁕

Feuilletage

....

[PUFF PASTRY]

....

Pâte feuilletée, or puff pastry dough, is the foundation for scores of French *pâtisseries*. The recipe is lengthy and involved, folding and rolling many times over to get a light flaky dough with literally hundreds of layers.

This flaky, buttery pastry is one of the glories of the French pastry chef's repertoire; the dough rises to about eight times its original height as it bakes. The process is time-consuming and involved but worth the effort. Prepare the dough one or two days before needed. This dough will keep for up to one week, tightly wrapped and refrigerated. It can also be frozen for up to one month.

3 CUPS/450 G ALL-PURPOSE
FLOUR

½ CUP/60 G CAKE FLOUR
(NOT SELF-RISING—IF UNAVAIL-
ABLE, USE A TOTAL OF
1 POUND/500 G ALL-PURPOSE
FLOUR)

2 TEASPOONS SALT

2 TABLESPOONS/30 G UNSALTED
BUTTER, MELTED AND COOLED

¼ CUP/60 ML MILK

¾ CUP/175 ML COLD WATER,
PLUS MORE IF NEEDED

1½ CUPS (¾ POUND)/350 G
UNSALTED BUTTER, CHILLED

BEFORE THE FIRST RISE, THE PÂTE FEUILLETÉE DOUGH IS CUT WITH AN X.

AFTER CHILLING, THE DOUGH IS ROLLED OUT INTO A SQUARISH SHAPE THAT CAN BE FOLDED INTO AN "ENVELOPE."

SET BUTTER INTO THE CENTER OF THE DOUGH AND FOLD ONE FLAP OF DOUGH OVER IT.

....

Combine the flours in a large mixing bowl or the bowl of an electric mixer and make a well in the center. Place the salt, melted butter, milk, and water in the center. Mix the ingredients together, either by hand or with an electric mixer, gradually incorporating the flour into the wet ingredients. Mix just until the ingredients come together to form a fairly firm dough; do not overwork. Add a spoonful or two more of water if the

FOLD THE REMAINING FLAPS OF DOUGH
OVER THE BUTTER AND SEAL IT IN.

LAYERS OF CHEESE AND HAM ARE SPREAD OVER THE PASTRY CRUST.

JEAN-LUC MARKS EACH "TURN"
WITH AN INDENTATION.

FOR THE PÂTE FEUILLETÉE AU
JAMBON ET FROMAGE, A CIRCLE OF
DOUGH IS PRESSED INTO THE BOT-
TOM OF A MOISTENED TART PAN.

A TOP CIRCLE OF DOUGH COVERS
THE HAM AND CHEESE FILLING,
AND THE CRUST IS THEN SEALED
AT THE EDGES.

JUST BEFORE BAKING, THE CRUST
IS PRICKED WITH A DIAMOND PAT-
TERN AND A SMALL CHEMINÉE, OR
VENT, IS ADDED TO RELEASE STEAM.

dough is too dry to come together. Place the dough in a mixing bowl and cut an X in the surface of the dough with a sharp knife. Cover with a kitchen towel or plastic wrap and refrigerate for 1 hour.

Take the butter out of the refrigerator and let stand for about 15 minutes at cool room temperature. Place the butter on a lightly floured sheet of plastic wrap. Sprinkle the butter lightly with flour and top with another sheet of plastic wrap.

Beat the butter with a rolling pin to soften it slightly; it should be malleable but still cool. Working quickly, with the palms of your hands, press the butter into a flat square about 5 inches/13 cm to a side and about ½ inch/1 cm thick. The dough and the butter should now be approximately the same consistency.

Lightly flour a work surface. Place the dough on the surface, flour it lightly, and press it into a square about 7 inches/18 cm and about 1

inch/2½ cm thick. With a rolling pin, roll the edges of the dough outward from the center, forming 4 flaps about 4 to 5 inches/10 to 12 cm long and about ¼ inch/½ cm thick.

Remove the top layer of plastic wrap and invert the square of butter onto the middle of the dough (see photo). Lift off the second layer of plastic wrap. Fold the 4 flaps of dough over the butter so that the edges all touch, making sure that it is sealed in.

Flour the work surface again

JEAN-LUC'S TARTE AUX POMMES RISSOLÉES, A SAUTÉED-APPLE TART, IS ENHANCED WITH A FILLING OF ALMOND CREAM.

lightly and sprinkle the package of dough with flour. Pat the dough gently with the length of the rolling pin at regular intervals, until it is about ½ inch/1 cm thick. Gently roll out the dough, using the rolling pin to roll the package smoothly without crushing it, forming a long rectangle about 8 x 20 inches/20 x 50 cm, with a short side closest to you. Try to keep the corners even as you roll.

Brush off any excess flour and fold the rectangle in thirds as you would a letter. Now rotate the package 90 degrees, so that the fold is at your left and the open side is at your right, similar to a book. (This process of rolling the dough into a rectangle, folding it in thirds, and rotating it 90 degrees is called a "single turn.") Wrap the dough in plastic, and refrigerate for at least 1 hour.

Give the dough 5 more single turns (place the dough on a lightly floured board with the fold at the left, the open side at the right); roll into a rectangle, fold in thirds, and rotate each time. Brush off any excess flour, then wrap and refrigerate the dough for at least 1 hour between each turn to let it rest. After the sixth turn, tightly wrap the dough and refrigerate overnight, or for at least 4 hours, before rolling out.

The dough is now ready to be rolled thin and cut as needed. When using puff pastry, be sure to cut straight down through the layers, using a large, very sharp knife so the dough will rise properly.

MAKES ABOUT 2½ POUNDS/1.14 KG

❋

Tarte aux Pommes Rissolées

·············

[SAUTÉED APPLE TART]

·············

This luscious variation on a classic apple tart features sautéed apples over a layer of almond cream.

2 TABLESPOONS/25 G BUTTER

1 VANILLA BEAN, CUT IN HALF LENGTHWISE WITH SEEDS SCOOPED OUT, OR 1 TEASPOON VANILLA EXTRACT

8 TO 9 GOLDEN DELICIOUS APPLES, PEELED, CUT INTO QUARTERS, AND CORED

½ RECIPE PUFF PASTRY, REFRIGERATED OVERNIGHT (PAGE 116)

·············

CRÈME D'AMANDES (ALMOND CREAM)

1 LARGE EGG

2 TABLESPOONS GROUND ALMONDS

2 TABLESPOONS VANILLA SUGAR, OR 2 TABLESPOONS SUGAR AND ¼ TEASPOON VANILLA EXTRACT

2 TABLESPOONS DARK RUM

Preheat the oven to 400°F./200°C. In a large skillet, melt the butter over medium heat, then stir in the vanilla. Add the apples, stirring to coat with the butter. Sauté, stirring frequently, until the apples are lightly browned, about 5 minutes. Remove from the heat and let cool.

On a lightly floured surface or between 2 sheets of wax paper, roll the puff pastry dough into a 12-inch/30-cm circle. Fit it without stretching into a 10-inch/25-cm tart pan that has been brushed with a pastry brush moistened in cold water. Press the dough gently in to the bottom and sides of the pan and pinch the edges around the top. Refrigerate, uncovered, until ready to use.

CRÈME D'AMANDES (ALMOND CREAM): In a small bowl, beat together the egg, almonds, vanilla sugar, and rum with a small whisk until thick and smooth.

Spread the almond cream over the bottom of the pastry shell. Arrange the apples over the cream in tight concentric circles so that almost no cream shows through. Bake on the center rack of the oven about 50 minutes, until the apples and crust are a deep golden brown. Cool on a wire rack. Serve lukewarm or at room temperature.

MAKES 6 TO 8 SERVINGS

·············

THE TARTES AUX PIGNONS, PINE-NUT TARTLETS, HERE SET ON AN OLD BAKER'S SCALE, ARE A VARIATION ON THE GÂTEAU BASQUE.

THE TARTES AUX FRAMBOISES EXEMPLIFY BASILE KAMIR'S STRAIGHTFORWARD WAY WITH PÂTISSERIE.

Pain Grenoblois

....

Tartes aux Framboises · Galette Charentaise

....

Fougasse · Baguette Parisienne

....

Coco au Miel

The tall, laconic Basile Kamir arrived at the firmament of top Paris bakers through an unusual and circuitous route. He began his working life as a journalist in the early 1970s, writing for the French news magazine *Actuèl*. From there he segued into organizing rock concerts and importing the latest releases from Virgin Records, owned by his childhood friend Richard Branson. Looking for inexpensive office space to house his rock and roll activities, he came upon a turn-of-the-century bakery that nobody wanted to rent, surrounded as it was by razed buildings on a site slated for a high-rise apartment complex. Basile moved into the little shop on the rue Vercingétorix, deep in the fourteenth arrondissement, and installed a couple of old barber's chairs so that clients could relax and listen to music. Shortly thereafter, friends suggested that it would be amusing for him to actually sell bread in the "bakery" so he made a deal with Lionel Poilâne to sell Poilâne bread alongside his records. By the late 1970s, this funky little enterprise began to unravel at the seams: Virgin Records, grown bigger and more corporate, took on a new importer; and Lionel Poilâne decided that Basile's rock and roll "hippie" environment gave his bread a bad image and ceased supplying his famous loaves.

This was the turning point for Basile and the inception of what would become one of the most appealing artisanal bakeries in Paris. Abandoning the world of pop music, Basile decided to return his shop to its original raison d'être by restoring it as a functioning *boulangerie*. He sought out and hired an

BASILE KAMIR'S APPEALING ASSORTMENT OF ARTISANAL BREADS FILLS AN
ANTIQUE RACK ON THE AVENUE DE SUFFREN.

. . . .

experienced baker to make breads in the old-fashioned, hand-crafted way, à la Poilâne in an old, wood-fired oven, and employed a young woman to sell them. Thus the Moulin de la Vierge was born, named for an ancient mill in the Aveyron region of south-central France where the Kamir family has a home. Shortly after this happy event, however, the building was scheduled for demolition, and the fight to save the bakery began, a battle with developers and government officials that was drawn-out and acrimonious but ultimately successful. Obstacles surpassed, Basile committed himself completely to learning everything he could about the métier of *boulanger,* working side by side for seven years with his master baker. Today the breads of Basile Kamir are always among the most highly rated in Paris.

There are three Moulin de la Vierge shops now, the original shop joined by another little shop on the rue Daguerre and by a large handsome *boulangerie à l'ancienne,* on the Avenue de Suffren, near the Eiffel Tower. All three shops are steeped in *nostalgie,* with panels of painting under glass, ornate moldings, and

trompe l'oeil tile flooring from the 1930s. Antique baker's racks are heaped with Basile's wonderful breads—the dense, chewy *pains de campagne,* his crisp, yeasty baguettes and *flûtes,* a rustic *Pain Grenoblois,* studded with walnuts and raisins, and an assortment of *fougasses*— lacy, cut-work breads in unusual shapes resembling trees or ladders and flavored with herbs or lardons, anchovies or cheese. Windows and marble counters display home-style *pâtisseries,* such as the *Coco au Miel,* chewy "coconut-ball" cupcakes; the *Galette Charentaise,* a giant, glazed shortbread butter cookie; and simple *Tartes aux Framboises,* piled with fresh summer raspberries.

Many of the breads from the Moulin de la Vierge are baked in the oldest functioning oven in Paris, dating from the turn of the century, a massive iron and brick Lefort that Basile discovered in the basement of the original shop. "An antique oven like this may not be as practical as a modern one—it takes three months to truly heat up and three months to cool down completely!" says Basile. "But the old bricks and the wood-fueled fire give bread

the best crust and the best flavor."

Basile's breads owe their flavor as well to the finest of raw materials. His organic flours, wheat and rye, are specially milled for him at an old mill with an antique stone south of Paris. "Bread is made from such simple components that each one must be top quality," Basile says. "The recipes for breads, as opposed to *pâtisseries,* are also very simple; so much depends on other factors—the temperature and the humidity of the environment, and on the expertise and the touch of the *boulanger.* A *boulanger* must live with his dough day to day, to touch it, to feel it often, controlling the fermentation, judging when the dough is ready. This is the art of the *boulanger.*"

❋

Pain Grenoblois

. . . .

[GRENOBLE RAISIN-NUT BREAD]

. . . .

This interesting bread incorporates two different kinds of dough, giving it a finer texture and a sweeter taste than a traditional country bread. It calls for a starter of *pâte Viennoise,* dough for an elegant, sweet milk bread, while the main body of dough includes rye, characteristic of a dense, rustic bread. This bread is delicious lightly toasted for breakfast, and is served as a dinner bread as well, cut in thin slices.

PÂTE VIENNOISE
STARTER

1 TEASPOON DRY YEAST

³/₄ CUP/175 ML WATER, AT ROOM
TEMPERATURE

2 ²/₃ CUP/340 G ALL-PURPOSE
UNBLEACHED FLOUR

1 TEASPOON SALT

2 TABLESPOONS SUGAR

4 TEASPOONS POWDERED
MILK

2 TABLESPOONS/25 G UNSALTED
BUTTER, AT COOL ROOM
TEMPERATURE, CUT INTO PIECES

. . . .

DOUGH

2 TABLESPOONS DRY YEAST

1¼ CUPS/310 ML WATER,
AT ROOM TEMPERATURE

3 CUPS/375 G ALL-PURPOSE
UNBLEACHED FLOUR

⅔ CUP/90 G RYE FLOUR

¼ CUP/50 G SUGAR

PINCH OF SALT

1 CUP/120 G CHOPPED WALNUTS

1 CUP/140 G RAISINS

PÂTE VIENNOISE STARTER: In a small bowl, combine the yeast with the water and stir to dissolve the yeast. Set aside for 5 minutes. In a large bowl, combine the flour, salt, sugar, and powdered milk. Pour in half the yeast-and-water mixture, and using your hands or a dough hook, begin to knead together the liquid and dry ingredients. After a minute, pour in the rest of the yeast-and-water mixture and continue kneading steadily in the bowl until

....

BASILE'S PAIN GRENOBLOIS, RICH WITH WALNUTS AND RAISINS, IS DELICIOUS SLICED FRESH FROM THE OVEN OR TOASTED THE NEXT DAY.

the dough is firm and elastic, about 5 minutes. If the dough is too sticky, sprinkle in a tablespoon or two of flour. Add the butter and knead another 2 minutes, or until the dough is satiny. Form into a ball and set into the center of the bowl. Cover the bowl with a towel and let rise for 45 minutes.

DOUGH: In a small bowl, combine the yeast and water, stirring to dissolve the yeast. In another bowl, mix the white flour, rye flour, sugar, salt, nuts, and raisins. Sprinkle this mixture evenly around the circumference of the ball of *pâte Viennoise* dough. Pour the yeast mixture over the circle of dry ingredients around the dough in a thin stream. Press both thumbs into the center of the dough and begin kneading the surrounding ingredients into the *pâte Viennoise*. After a minute, turn the dough out onto a floured work surface or transfer to an electric mixer with a dough hook and continue kneading for 10 to 15 minutes, until the dough is supple and elastic. If the dough is too sticky, sprinkle with a bit of white flour; if the dough is too dense, sprinkle in about a tablespoon or two of water at room temperature. Form the dough into a ball, place in a large greased bowl, cover with a cloth, and let rise in a draft-free place 1½ hours, or until doubled in volume.

Preheat the oven to 400°F./200°C for 20 minutes. Place a small metal baking pan of hot water on the floor of the oven. Form the dough into 2 rings about 10 inches/25 cm in diameter or 2 long free-form rectangular loaves about 13 inches/33 cm long, or divide into 2 greased 8-inch/20-cm loaf pans. Remove the hot water. Bake the breads on greased baking sheets on the bottom rack of the oven for 30 to 40 minutes, until the loaves are well browned. Cool the rings or free-form loaves directly on wire racks; cool the pan loaves in the pans on wire racks. These breads, while of course best on

the day they are baked, remain fresh 2 or 3 days wrapped in foil.

SERVES 6 TO 8

❋

Tartes aux

Framboises

....

[RASPBERRY TARTLETS]

....

To enjoy this simple, rich pastry at its crispest, assemble these tarts shortly before serving them. If they sit too long filled with cream and fresh fruit they will become soggy.

PÂTE SUCRÉE

1½ CUPS PLUS 1 TABLE-
SPOON/220 G ALL-PURPOSE
FLOUR

¼ CUP PLUS 3 TABLESPOONS/
90 G SUGAR

7 TABLESPOONS/100 G UNSALTED
BUTTER, CUT INTO PIECES

2 LARGE EGGS, WELL BEATEN

....

FILLING

1 TO 1½ CUPS/250 TO 375 ML
PASTRY CREAM (PAGE 00)

3 CUPS/375 G RASPBERRIES

CONFECTIONERS' SUGAR,
FOR SPRINKLING

PÂTE SUCRÉE: Combine the flour and sugar in a mixing bowl or food processor. Add the butter and cut the mixture together until crumbly. Add the eggs and mix or pulse just until the dough comes together. Gather the dough into a ball, flatten into a disk shape, and wrap in plastic. Refrigerate at least 1 hour.

Roll the dough out on a lightly floured work surface to a thickness of slightly less than ⅛ inch/⅓ cm. Use a 4-inch/10-cm biscuit cutter or saucer to cut rounds of dough. Fit the rounds without stretching into the bottoms and sides of 8 to 10 buttered shallow 3½- to 4-inch/9- to 10-cm tartlet pans. Chill the dough,

IN HIS SHOP ON THE RUE VERCINGÉTORIX, BASILE KAMIR BAKES BREAD IN THE OLDEST WOOD-FIRED OVEN IN PARIS.

uncovered, for at least 15 minutes.

Preheat the oven to 400°F./200°C. Place the tart shells on a baking sheet and prick the pastry gently with a fork. Line each shell with a small buttered piece of aluminum foil, buttered side down. Bake until the pastry is golden and baked through, about 15 minutes. Transfer the baking sheet to a wire rack and carefully remove the foil linings. Cool the pastry shells completely.

FILLING: Shortly before serving, remove the pastry shells from the tart pans. Spoon the pastry cream into the cooled pastry shells, filling them about one-third full. Arrange the raspberries on top. Sprinkle with confectioners' sugar and serve.

MAKES 8 TO 10 TARTLETS

❋

Galette Charentaise

. . . .

[CHARENTE-STYLE WAFER
COOKIE]

. . . .

Shortbread *galettes* are popular, traditional cookies in Brittany and fur-

ther south in the Charente, which gives its name to this cookie. Basile Kamir offers this super-sized variation in his shop.

1 ³/₄ CUPS/250 G ALL-PURPOSE
FLOUR

¹/₂ CUP/125 G UNSALTED BUTTER,
AT ROOM TEMPERATURE, CUT
INTO PIECES

¹/₂ CUP/100 G SUGAR

¹/₄ TEASPOON SALT

1 TABLESPOON COLD WATER

1 LARGE EGG YOLK, WELL-BEATEN
WITH 1 TEASPOON WATER, FOR
GLAZE

1 TABLESPOON SLICED BLANCHED
ALMONDS

Place the flour in a mixing bowl. Make a well in the center and add the butter, sugar, salt, and water. With your fingertips, mix the butter with the other ingredients, gradually incorporating the flour until the dough comes together. Gather the dough into a ball, flatten it slightly into a disk shape, and wrap it in plastic. Refrigerate at least ¹/₂ hour.

Preheat the oven to 350°F./175°C. On a lightly floured surface, roll the dough out to an 8-inch/20-cm circle about ¹/₂ inch/1 cm thick. With a paring knife, score the edges at regular

intervals to create a scalloped edge. Carefully transfer the round of dough to a buttered baking sheet or a sheet lined with parchment paper. Brush the surface of the dough with the egg yolk mixture to glaze evenly. With the tines of a fork, trace a crisscross pattern in the egg glaze; then sprinkle the almonds over the surface.

Bake the *galette* until golden brown, 25 to 27 minutes. Cool the pan on a wire rack; then transfer the *galette* to a doily-lined serving plate.

MAKES ONE 8-INCH/20-CM COOKIE

❋

Fougasse

. . . .

[LACY BAGUETTE]

. . . .

This *pain de fantaisie*, cut out and pulled into various shapes such as a ladder or a tree, is usually made from baguette dough and is often flavored with lardons of bacon, grated cheese, herbs, onions, or anchovies.

1 RECIPE BAGUETTE PARISIENNE;
ADD THE DESIRED FLAVORING
INGREDIENT BELOW WITH THE
FLOUR AND SALT AND PREPARE
THROUGH THE FIRST RISE
(PAGE 126)

1 CUP/250 G CUBED COOKED
SLAB BACON

¹/₂ TEASPOON FRESHLY GROUND
PEPPER

OR

1 CUP/250 G GRATED GRUYÈRE
CHEESE

¹/₄ TEASPOON WHITE PEPPER

OR

1 TABLESPOON HERBES DE
PROVENCE (DRIED FINES HERBES)

OR

4 ANCHOVY FILLETS, RINSED
AND CHOPPED

UNBLEACHED ALL-PURPOSE
FLOUR, FOR SPRINKLING

After the first rising of the flavored baguette dough, punch down and divide the dough in 2 pieces. On a floured work surface, roll out one-half of the dough to a long, very flat rectangle, about 8 x 15 inches/20 x 38 cm and ¹/₂ inch/1 cm thick.

. . . .

A GIANT ALMOND-TOPPED SHORTBREAD COOKIE, THE GALETTE CHARENTAISE,
ORIGINATED IN THE CHARENTE REGION SOUTH OF BRITTANY.

BASILE CREATES HIS FOUGASSE
BREADS IN A VARIETY OF INTRIGU-
ING LACY SHAPES AND FLAVORS.

....

For a ladder shape, make a series of 4 horizontal cuts about 3 inches/8 cm wide and 3 inches/8 cm apart down the center of the rectangle, cutting completely through the dough. (Be careful *not* to cut through the edges, or the perimeter, of the bread, which acts as the frame.) With your hands, pull the dough gently apart vertically so that the cuts open to rectangular spaces. Repeat with the other half of the dough.

For a tree shape, form the dough into a rough triangular shape, stretching the bottom gently, then roll out flat to a thickness of about ½ inch/1 cm. On either side of an imaginary center "trunk," cut 3 diagonal slashes through the dough, as though you were drawing the branches of a stick Christmas tree, again being careful not to cut through the sides of the dough. Gently pull the cuts apart to accentuate the tree and branch shape. Repeat with the other half of the dough. Gently transfer the breads to lightly greased baking sheets, taking care to retain their shapes. Cover loosely with plastic wrap and let rise 1½ hours.

Preheat the oven to 450°F./230°C. Dust the breads lightly with flour. Place a baking pan of hot water on the floor of the oven. Bake the breads on the bottom and center racks of the oven for 15 minutes. Remove the water. Reduce the temperature to 400°F./200°C and switch the baking sheets on the racks. Bake another 10 minutes, or until golden brown. Cool on wire racks.

MAKES 2 LARGE, LACY BREADS

❋

Baguette Parisienne

....

This classic French bread, whose image instantly signifies France, originated in Paris in the mid-1800s. It was probably inspired by the long, thin *pain Viennois*, a sweet bread made with sugar and milk by a group of Austrian bakers who had immigrated to Paris and set up shop at the time. The French baguette is simply made of white flour, water, yeast, and salt, and undergoes very little fermentation. It is meant to be eaten within a couple of hours after baking. It self-destructs within a few hours, losing its moisture and freshness and becoming hard and inedible. This dough can be chilled after the first rising, wrapped in plastic wrap, for 24 to 48 hours, so you can use half one day and the rest another. If chilled, remove from the refrigerator an hour before working it. Then punch down and form in baguettes, rolls, or a ring.

1 ¾ CUPS/425 ML WATER AT ROOM
TEMPERATURE

1 TABLESPOON DRY YEAST

4 ¼ CUPS/560 G HARD WHEAT OR
ALL-PURPOSE UNBLEACHED
WHITE FLOUR

1 TABLESPOON SALT, PREFER-
ABLY SEA SALT

In a small bowl, combine the water and yeast, stirring well to dissolve the yeast. Set aside 5 minutes. Combine the flour and salt in a large bowl, then pour in the yeast mixture in a thin stream, stirring as you pour. Mix

slowly, either with an electric mixer equipped with a dough hook or with your hands, for 15 minutes. If hand kneading, transfer the dough to a floured work surface when it holds together in a single mass. When the dough is smooth, supple, and elastic, form it into a ball and center it in a clean bowl, then cover with a cloth and let rise in a draft-free place for 1 hour, or until doubled.

Divide the dough into 4 parts. Knead each piece thoroughly on a lightly floured work surface, squashing it flat with the heel of your hand over and over again for about 2 minutes to squeeze out built-up gases. Form each piece by pressing it out into a flat rectangle, about 5 x 9 inches/13 x 23 cm. (Fold a 3-inch/8-cm flap from one short end of the dough into the center and press down. Fold the other end over the first fold, covering it, and press down. Do 2 more folds of the dough in upon itself, working always from the short end so that the dough resembles a thick,

....

THE CLASSIC BAGUETTE DOUGH
CAN BE FASHIONED INTO MANY
SHAPES, INCLUDING THIS BRAIDED
LOAF WOVEN FROM THREE THIN
STRANDS OF DOUGH.

stumpy hot dog roll.) With your 2 palms together on top of the center of the dough, begin rolling the dough back and forth under your hands, slowly elongating the roll of dough into a long, skinny baguette shape, about 14 inches/35 cm long and 2 inches/5 cm wide. Repeat for each of the other 3 pieces. Set the 4 baguettes close together on a floured linen or cotton (not terry) towel, separating each with a fold of fabric between them from end to end. Cover with another towel and let rise for 45 minutes. Form the dough into the desired shape just before the final rising (see variations below).

Preheat the oven to 450°F./230°C. Place a small metal pan filled with hot water on the floor of the oven to approximate the moist environment of French baking ovens. Transfer the baguettes into baguette pans, onto lightly greased baking sheets, or, if using baking stones, onto a *pelle*, or peel, the long-handled, flat-bladed "shovel" used by bakers (and pizza makers) to place breads directly into the oven. Make a series of shallow diagonal cuts across the tops of the baguettes with a *lame*, or single-edge razor, about every 2 inches. This allows gases and moisture to escape from the baking breads and makes a nice pattern in the finished crust. Place the breads in the center of the oven and bake for 15 minutes. Remove the pan of water. Lower the temperature to 400°F./200°C. and bake another 8 to 10 minutes, until golden brown. Cool on a wire rack. Serve within 3 hours or wrap well and freeze when lukewarm.

VARIATION: This versatile dough can also be divided into 3 strips and braided; formed into a ring; formed into skinny 10-inch/25-cm sticks; formed into 2 large baguettes; shaped into small round dinner rolls; or stretched and patted into one long classic baguette.

MAKES 4 THIN
"FICELLE" BAGUETTES

DENSE, CHEWY, AND DELICIOUS, THE COCOS AU MIEL, COCONUT-HONEY CAKES, ADD A TROPICAL TOUCH TO WINDOWS AT TRADITIONAL PÂTISSERIES.

Coco au Miel

[COCONUT-HONEY CAKES]

1¼ CUPS/310 ML MILK

1¼ TEASPOONS HONEY

3 CUPS/230 G SHREDDED
COCONUT

½ CUP/125 G SUGAR

½ CUP/70 G ALL-PURPOSE FLOUR

2 TEASPOONS BAKING POWDER

2 LARGE EGGS, WELL BEATEN

Preheat the oven to 400°F./200°C. Line 10 muffin tins with paper baking cup liners and set the pan aside.

In a heavy saucepan, bring the milk and honey to a boil over medium heat, then remove from the heat.

In a mixing bowl, combine the coconut, sugar, flour, and baking powder. Slowly add the milk mixture and stir until smooth. Stir in the eggs until well combined; the mixture will be quite liquid. Pour the mixture into the paper cups, filling them nearly full. Each time you fill a cup, give the mixture a stir to redistribute the coconut.

Bake until the cakes are golden brown and a toothpick inserted in the center emerges clean, about 25 to 30 minutes. Cool in the pan on a wire rack.

MAKES ABOUT 10 CAKES

AT HIS SAINT-GERMAIN SHOP, GÉRARD MULOT STANDS BEHIND A COLORFUL TRAY OF HIS SIGNATURE MACARONS.

Tourte au Saumon · Tarte au Citron

....

Galette à l'Orange

....

Charlotte aux Framboises · Macarons

....

Quiche aux Courgettes et Tomates

....

Brioches aux Gouttes de Chocolat

As a young boy growing up in a little village in Alsace-Lorraine, Gérard Mulot never dreamed he would one day be creating croissants and exquisite *pâtisseries* for Catherine Deneuve, Marcello Mastroianni, and a pride of France's distinguished *sénateurs*. His heart's desire at the age of fourteen was to be a restaurant cook. "But when it came time to look for an apprenticeship in a restaurant kitchen," recalls this genial, soft-spoken man, born into a modest farming family, "there was nothing available. It was disappointing. The only opening I could find was in a *boulangerie* as a baker's apprentice. So I took that, always, though, with the hope of coming back to cuisine." As it happened, he has remained in the domain of baking longer than he ever imagined, becoming one of Paris's elite *pâtissiers* while still in his thirties.

At eighteen, he left the Vosges for Paris, where he worked in a variety of small shops, turning out breads and simple pastries before he joined the august house of Dalloyau "to perfect my *pâtisserie.*" In 1975, longing for his own place and greater artistic freedom, he rented a small *pâtisserie* dating from the 1930s in the sixth arrondissement of the Quartier Latin, across the rue Lobineau from the handsome Souleiado fabric boutique and a short walk from the French *Sénat* in the Luxembourg Palace. It is this space he eventually bought and expanded into his current *pâtisserie,* a dazzling and pristine emporium

CHOOSING ONE CAKE OR TART FROM THE WINDOW OF GÉRARD MULOT'S
SHOP IS A DELICIOUSLY AGONIZING DECISION.

....

that is rarely without a line snaking out the door.

The Gérard Mulot *Pâtisserie* is a large and thriving operation with twenty-four people working just in the downstairs *laboratoire,* or pastry kitchen, two bakers in the *boulangerie* area, and two *chocolatiers* devoting themselves exclusively to the production of chocolates up in an airy room above the shop. Managing the marbled and mirrored front of the shop is Madame Mulot, Marie-Claude, whom Gérard met shortly after his arrival in Paris when he was producing breads and *pâtisseries* behind the scenes in a small boulangerie and she was selling the finished products up front. For Monsieur Mulot the day begins at 5:00 A.M. when he sets to work on the breakfast croissants and brioches, some of which he personally delivers at 8:00 A.M. to nearby offices and hotels. It is in this area of *viennoiserie* that Monsieur Mulot first developed one of his specialties—the *Brioches aux Gouttes de Chocolat,* his irresistible chocolate chip brioches, which sell both as a breakfast pastry and as an after-school treat for chil-

dren. Among the *pâtisserie* highlights are beautiful cakes and tarts made with the fresh fruits bought daily at the Rungis market outside of Paris. Monsieur Mulot is also celebrated for his pastel-hued *macarons,* variously flavored with chocolate, strawberry, coffee, pistachio, or vanilla.

I have an old friend who has long worked near the *Sénat;* she is a beautiful, elegant, and exceedingly slim woman whose only *gourmandise,* or weakness, is a single large *macaron* from Mulot almost every day after lunch before returning to her office. One warm spring afternoon in the mid-1970s, I happily accompanied her to Mulot's original little shop and had my first *macaron*—a vanilla one. The sensory memory of biting into that fragile combination of egg white, powdered almonds, and sugar—teeth sinking through the delicate exterior with the barely resistant quality of a quail's eggshell, into the delicate, chewy interior, and finally down into the almond butter cream that binds the two halves together—remains with me, intensely, to this day.

Tourte au Saumon

....

[SALMON QUICHE]

....

Gérard Mulot cures the salmon similarly to gravlax, seasoning the fish and refrigerating it overnight. This method has been adapted slightly, with the salmon being cooked thoroughly before it is added to the quiche.

PÂTE À QUICHE

1/2 CUP (1 STICK)/125 G UNSALT-
ED BUTTER, SOFTENED

1 2/3 CUPS/230 G ALL-PURPOSE
FLOUR

1/2 CUP/75 G CORNSTARCH

1 1/2 TEASPOONS SALT

1/4 CUP/60 ML WATER

4 LARGE EGG YOLKS

....

FILLING

6 TO 8 OUNCES/175 TO 250 G
SALMON FILLET OR STEAK, SKIN
AND BONES REMOVED, CUT IN
1/2-INCH/1-CM CUBES

1 TEASPOON SALT, PLUS MORE
AS NEEDED

3/4 TEASPOON SUGAR

1 TEASPOON WHITE PEPPER,
OR TO TASTE

1/2 TEASPOON GROUND
FENNEL SEEDS

4 TABLESPOONS/
60 G UNSALTED BUTTER

2 1/2 CUPS/75 G TRIMMED FRESH
SPINACH, WASHED WELL
(OR 1/3 10-OUNCE/300-G PACKAGE
FROZEN SPINACH, THAWED
AND SQUEEZED DRY)

1 CUP/150 G SLICED WILD
MUSHROOMS (SUCH AS CEPES
OR SHIITAKES) OR DOMESTIC
MUSHROOM CAPS

1/3 CUP/120 G DICED SEEDED
RIPE TOMATO

2 1/2 OUNCES/75 G SMOKED
SALMON, CHOPPED

4 LARGE EGGS

1 CUP/250 ML CRÈME FRAÎCHE
OR HEAVY CREAM

3/4 CUP/175 ML MILK

2 TABLESPOONS CHOPPED
FRESH DILL, PLUS SEVERAL
SMALL SPRIGS

PÂTE À QUICHE: Place the butter in a mixing bowl or food processor. Add the flour and cornstarch, gradually incorporating them into the butter without handling the mixture too roughly. Dissolve the salt in the water and add to the bowl along with the egg yolks. Mix or pulse gently until the dough comes together. Flatten the dough into a disk shape, wrap in plastic, and chill at least 1 hour before using.

Roll the dough on a lightly floured work surface to a thickness of about ⅛ inch/⅓ cm. Fit the dough without stretching into a buttered 9-inch/23-cm springform pan, a deep 9-inch/23-cm tart pan, or an 11 x 1¼-inch/28 x 3-cm false-bottomed quiche or tart pan, forming an even side 1 inch/2½-cm high and trim-ming the edges. Chill the pastry shell at least ½ hour.

FILLING: Place the salmon cubes in a non-aluminum bowl or container; sprinkle with the salt, sugar, ¼ teaspoon white pepper, and the fennel seeds. Cover with plastic wrap and marinate in the refrigerator for at least 3 hours, stirring once or twice.

Preheat the oven to 400°F./200°C. Place the pastry shell on a baking sheet. Line the shell with parchment paper or lightly buttered aluminum foil and fill with dried beans or rice. Bake until the sides have set, about 10 minutes. Carefully remove the paper and beans and continue to bake until the pastry is very pale gold but not yet baked through, 7 or 8 minutes longer. Remove from the oven and set aside on a wire rack, leaving the oven on.

Meanwhile, heat 1½ tablespoons of the butter in a large skillet over medium-low heat. Add the spinach, sprinkle with salt and ¼ teaspoon white pepper, and cook, tossing, just until wilted but still bright green, about 30 seconds. Transfer the spinach to a strainer and set aside to cool. Gently press the spinach with a wooden spoon to drain excess liquid, then chop the spinach and set aside.

Add 1½ tablespoons of butter to the skillet and raise the heat to medium-high. Add the mushrooms, season with salt and ¼ teaspoon white pepper, and sauté, tossing, until wilted and beginning to brown, about 4 minutes. Transfer to the strainer and set aside to cool.

Add the remaining 1 tablespoon of butter to the skillet over medium-high heat, then add the salmon cubes. Sauté over medium heat, tossing, just until opaque, about 1 or 2 minutes.

Scatter the spinach in the partially baked pastry, then distribute the mushrooms over the spinach. Scatter the salmon cubes over, then the tomato and sprinkle lightly with salt. Scatter the smoked salmon on top. In a mixing bowl, whisk together the eggs, crème fraîche, milk, chopped dill, salt to taste, and remaining ¼ teaspoon white pepper. Place the pan on the center oven rack and gently pour the egg mixture into the pastry shell. Sprinkle the dill sprigs on top.

Bake until the custard has just set and is lightly golden, about 30 minutes (the timing can vary based on the depth of the pan; do not overbake). To test, jiggle the pan gently; the custard will be set if the center doesn't move. Carefully remove the sides of the pan and cool the quiche briefly on a wire rack. Serve warm.

MAKES ONE 9- TO 11-INCH/ 23- TO 28-CM QUICHE

MULOT'S TORTE AU SAUMON IS A TANTALIZING COMPOSITION OF SALMON, TOMATOES, DILL, MUSHROOMS, AND SPINACH.

Tarte au Citron

....

[LEMON TART]

....

½ RECIPE PÂTE SABLÉE,
CHILLED (SEE BELOW)

....

CRÈME AU CITRON (LEMON CREAM)

¾ CUP/175 ML FRESH LEMON
JUICE (ABOUT 5 OR 6 LEMONS)

10 TABLESPOONS
(1 ¼ STICKS)/150 G UNSALTED
BUTTER, AT ROOM TEMPERATURE,
CUT INTO PIECES

1 CUP/200 G SUGAR

2 LARGE EGGS

3 LARGE EGG YOLKS

Roll the *pâte sablée* dough between 2 sheets of wax paper or on a lightly floured work surface to a thickness of slightly less than ⅛ inch/⅓ cm. (Reserve the remaining dough for another use.) Fit the pastry without stretching into a 9-inch/23-cm false-bottomed tart pan, or into a flan ring that has been placed on a baking sheet covered with a sheet of parchment paper or lightly greased. Trim the edges of the pastry and

....

A BRIGHT YELLOW CIRCLE OF
INTENSE LEMON ESSENCE, MULOT'S
TARTE AU CITRON IS ONE OF THE
BEST LEMON TARTS IN PARIS.

refrigerate for at least ½ hour.

Preheat the oven to 400°F./200°C. Place the pastry-lined tart pan on a baking sheet. Line the shell with parchment paper or lightly buttered aluminum foil and fill with dried beans or rice. Bake until the sides have set, about 10 minutes. Carefully remove the paper and beans and continue to bake until the shell is very pale gold but not yet baked through, about 8 minutes longer.

CRÈME AU CITRON (LEMON CREAM): In a large nonaluminum saucepan or casserole, heat the lemon juice, butter, and ¾ cup/150 g of the sugar over low heat until the butter has melted and the mixture comes to a gentle simmer, about 2 minutes. Meanwhile, with an electric mixer, beat the eggs, egg yolks, and remaining ¼ cup/50 g sugar at medium-high speed until the mixture is pale and light, about 4 minutes. Lower the mixer speed and slowly pour the hot lemon juice mixture into the egg mixture, beating until blended and fluffy, about 3 minutes. Return the mixture to the saucepan and cook over medium-low heat, stirring constantly with a wooden spoon until the mixture nearly starts to simmer, about 3 minutes. Transfer the lemon cream to a metal mixing bowl and refrigerate until cool. If not using immediately, lay a sheet of plastic wrap or wax paper directly on the surface of the cream.

With a rubber spatula, spread the cooled lemon cream evenly into the pastry shell; it should nearly fill the shell. Smooth the top with the spatula. Return the tart to the oven and bake 5 minutes longer, which will set the filling slightly without coloring it. Carefully remove the edges of the tart pan and cool the tart on a wire rack. Refrigerate the tart until the filling is firm. Remove the tart from the refrigerator 10 or 15 minutes before serving. This tart, like all pastry desserts, is best served on the day it is baked.

SERVES 6 TO 8

Galette à l'Orange

....

[ORANGE TART]

....

Monsieur Mulot says that this tart is ideal as an accompaniment to a cup of tea. The rich dough is somewhat difficult to handle; it is easiest to roll on a lightly floured sheet of wax paper. This recipe makes double the amount of dough you need for the crust, but the pastry is very versatile and nice to have on hand.

PÂTE SABLÉE

1 ½ CUPS (1 ¾ STICKS)/200 G
UNSALTED BUTTER, SOFTENED

⅔ CUP/90 G CONFECTIONERS'
SUGAR

1 LARGE EGG, BEATEN

½ TEASPOON SALT

½ TEASPOON VANILLA EXTRACT
(OR ¾ TEASPOON VANILLA
SUGAR)

1 ¾ CUPS/250 G ALL-PURPOSE
FLOUR

2 TABLESPOONS GROUND
BLANCHED ALMONDS

....

FILLING

⅓ CUP/110 G BITTER ORANGE
MARMALADE

2 LARGE EGG WHITES

3 ½ TABLESPOONS SUGAR

2 TABLESPOONS GROUND
BLANCHED ALMONDS

1 ¾ TEASPOONS ALL-PURPOSE
FLOUR

CONFECTIONERS' SUGAR,
FOR SPRINKLING

5 DIAMOND-SHAPED PIECES
CANDIED ORANGE RIND
(OPTIONAL)

PÂTE SABLÉE: In a large mixing bowl or food processor, combine the butter, confectioners' sugar, egg, salt, and vanilla and mix until blended. Sift the flour, then gradually add it to the butter mixture along with the almonds. Don't mix too vigorously, or the pastry will toughen. When the dough comes together, divide it in half and form each into a disk shape. Wrap each piece of pastry in plastic and chill overnight, or at least 1 hour.

Remove 1 piece of pastry from the

A MULOT SPECIALTY AND PERENNIAL FAVORITE AT THE SHOP, THE GALETTE À L'ORANGE MARRIES THE FLAVORS OF BITTER ORANGE AND SWEET ALMOND MERINGUE.

. . . .

sheet of aluminum foil, buttered side down. Bake the crust until the sides have set, about 10 minutes. Carefully remove the foil.

FILLING: With a spoon or spatula, spread the marmalade over the bottom of the pastry shell. In a large mixing bowl, beat the egg whites until they are frothy. Gradually add 1½ tablespoons of the sugar and continue to beat until the whites form stiff but not dry peaks. Meanwhile, sift the ground almonds, remaining 2 tablespoons sugar, and flour onto a sheet of wax or parchment paper. Gently fold this mixture into the egg whites with a large rubber spatula. Gently spread this mixture evenly over the marmalade and sprinkle lightly with confectioners' sugar. If you like, arrange the candied orange lozenges around the edge.

Bake the *galette* for about 20 minutes, or until the pastry and the meringue are pale golden. Cool to room temperature on a wire rack, then sprinkle again with confectioners' sugar and serve in wedges.

SERVES 6 TO 8

❄

*Charlotte
aux Framboises*

. . . .

[RASPBERRY CHARLOTTE]

. . . .

The ladyfingers in this recipe are made from scratch, just as they are by Gérard Mulot. You may choose to substitute commercially produced ladyfingers to save some time and effort.

BISCUIT À LA CUILLÈRE
(LADYFINGERS)

¾ CUP (SCANT)/100 G
ALL-PURPOSE FLOUR

4 LARGE EGGS, SEPARATED

¼ CUP PLUS 3 TABLESPOONS/
90 G SUGAR

CONFECTIONERS' SUGAR

. . . .

refrigerator, reserving the other for another use. Place the pastry on a lightly floured sheet of wax paper; dust the pastry with flour and roll to an 11-inch/28-cm circle with a thickness of about ⅛ inch/⅓ cm. Invert the pastry without stretching onto a buttered 8- or 9-inch/20- or 23-cm false-bottomed tart pan.

Carefully peel off the wax paper. Trim off the excess dough and form a neat high rim. Gently press the dough between your thumb and forefinger at regular intervals, forming a rippled border. Refrigerate the pastry shell, uncovered, for at least ½ hour.

Preheat the oven to 350°F./175°C. Line the pastry shell with a buttered

AN EPHEMERAL WORK OF THE PÂTISSIER'S ART, MULOT'S CHARLOTTE AUX FRAMBOISES TESTIFIES TO HIS FINESSE.

CRÈME BAVAROISE

(BAVARIAN CREAM)

1 CUP/250 ML MILK

¼ CUP PLUS 2 TABLESPOONS/
85 G SUGAR

½ VANILLA BEAN, SPLIT LENGTH-
WISE, OR 2 TEASPOONS PURE
VANILLA EXTRACT

2 TABLESPOONS COLD WATER

2 TEASPOONS (4 SHEETS)
PLAIN GELATIN

3 LARGE EGG YOLKS

....

ASSEMBLY

2 TABLESPOONS FRAMBOISE
(CLEAR RASPBERRY BRANDY),
OR TO TASTE

4 CUPS/500 G FRESH
RASPBERRIES

¾ CUP/175 ML HEAVY CREAM,
WELL CHILLED

COULIS DE FRAMBOISE
(RECIPE FOLLOWS)

3 TABLESPOONS RED CURRANT
JELLY OR STRAINED RASPBERRY
PRESERVES, OR AS NEEDED

BISCUIT À LA CUILLÈRE (LADY-
FINGERS): Preheat the oven to
350°F./175°C. Line a baking sheet
with parchment paper, or, alternatively butter and flour the baking
sheet. Sift the flour onto a sheet of
wax paper and set aside. In a large
bowl, beat the egg whites until they
form soft peaks. Gradually add the
sugar and continue to beat until they
are stiff but not dry. In a small bowl,
stir the egg yolks until smooth, then
gently fold the egg yolks into the
meringue until nearly blended. Add
the flour in a thin stream, folding
gently just until incorporated.

Place the batter in a pastry bag
with a ½-inch/1-cm plain tip (or use
a bag without a tip). Holding the bag
at a 45-degree angle to the pan, with
the tip touching the paper, pipe out
about 30 fingers about 2½ inches/6
cm long, piping them diagonally on
the parchment, parallel to each other
(the ladyfingers will not spread during baking). Pull up the tip of the
pastry bag at the end of each finger
to form a neat finger shape. Sift a
generous coating of confectioners'
sugar over the fingers.

Bake until the ladyfingers are
golden and spring back when pressed
gently, about 17 minutes. Cool the
pan briefly on a wire rack; then use a
spatula to gently transfer the biscuits
to the rack and cool completely.

CRÈME BAVAROISE (BAVARIAN
CREAM): Place the milk, 2 tablespoons sugar, and the vanilla bean in
a large heavy saucepan. Bring to a
boil, remove from the heat, cover,
and set aside at least ½ hour to
infuse. Place the water in a small cup
or bowl and sprinkle the gelatin over.
Set aside for about 5 minutes.

Return the milk mixture to a simmer over low heat. In a large nonaluminum mixing bowl, whisk the egg
yolks with ¼ cup/50 g sugar until
pale, about 4 minutes. Slowly pour
the hot milk mixture onto the egg
yolk mixture, whisking vigorously.
Return the mixture to the saucepan
and cook over low heat, stirring constantly with a wooden spoon until the
mixture thickens lightly, about 3
minutes. Do not allow the mixture to
boil. Remove from the heat and stir
in the gelatin until dissolved (add the
vanilla extract now, if you are using
it). Strain the mixture into a clean
bowl and refrigerate for ½ hour to 1
hour, stirring now and then, until the
mixture is cool and beginning to
thicken but has not yet set, about the
consistency of raw egg whites.

ASSEMBLY: Line the outside edge of
an 8- or 8 ½-inch/20- or 21-cm
springform pan—Monsieur Mulot
uses a bottomless flan ring about 2 ¼
inches/6 cm deep, placing it on a
round of cardboard or a serving platter—with whole ladyfingers, their
rounded tops facing outward. As you
fit them around the pan or flan ring,
use a serrated knife to trim the tops
of the ladyfingers so that when they
stand up, they are flush with the top
edge of the pan. Line the bottom of
the pan with more ladyfingers, using
any irregularly shaped ladyfingers
for the base. Brush the bottom layer
and upright sides of the ladyfingers
with framboise.

Set aside and refrigerate 3 cups/
375 g of the best-looking raspberries
for the garnish. Whip the cream
until it forms soft peaks. Immediately fold the cream gently into the
Bavarian cream base. Pour about
one-third of the Bavarian mixture
into the ring. Scatter about ½
cup/160 g of the remaining raspberries over the cream. Pour another
one-third of the cream over the
berries, then scatter ½ cup berries
over. Fill with the remaining cream.
Loosely cover the pan with plastic
wrap and refrigerate the Bavarian
overnight, or for at least 6 hours.

Prepare the *Coulis de Framboise.*
Shortly before serving, arrange the
reserved raspberries to completely
cover the surface of the Bavarian
cream, piling them higher than the
ladyfingers. In a small saucepan,
warm the red currant jelly or
strained raspberry preserves over low
heat just until melted and gently
brush the top layer of berries with a
light glaze of jelly. Carefully remove
the sides of the springform pan or
lift off the flan ring. If you like, tie a
ribbon around the ladyfingers for
presentation. Serve the Bavarian cut
in wedges, pouring some raspberry
coulis alongside each serving.

SERVES ABOUT 8

❋

Coulis de Framboise

....

[RASPBERRY SAUCE]

....

1 PINT/500 G FRESH RASP-
BERRIES, WASHED

⅓ CUP/75 G SUGAR, PREFERABLY
SUPERFINE, OR MORE TO TASTE

Puree the berries with the sugar in a
blender or food processor until
smooth. Press the mixture through a
sieve to remove seeds. Refrigerate
the puree in a sauceboat or small
serving bowl, covered, until needed.
The *coulis* can be prepared up to 2
days ahead.

THE PRISTINE GLASS DISPLAY
CASES IN MULOT'S SPOTLESS SHOP
OFFER A CORNUCOPIA OF PREPARED
ENTRÉES AND SALADS AS WELL AS
HIS FAMOUS PASTRIES.

Macarons

[VANILLA-ALMOND MACAROONS]

MACAROONS

1¼ CUPS PLUS 2 TABLE-
SPOONS/100 G SLICED BLANCHED
ALMONDS

1⅓ CUPS/200 G CONFECTIONERS'
SUGAR

6 LARGE EGG WHITES, AT ROOM
TEMPERATURE

¼ CUP/50 G SUGAR

FILLING

⅓ CUP/100 G ALMOND PASTE

3½ TABLESPOONS/50 G UNSALTED
BUTTER, SOFTENED

½ TEASPOON VANILLA EXTRACT

MACAROONS: Preheat the oven to 400°F./200°C. In a food processor, grind the almonds and confectioners' sugar until powdery. Sift onto a sheet of wax paper.

Beat the egg whites until they are frothy. Gradually add the sugar and continue to beat until the whites are stiff but not dry. With a large rubber spatula, gently and gradually fold the almond mixture into the egg whites until well combined.

Line a baking sheet with parchment paper, then place it on top of another baking sheet, which will prevent the bottoms of the macaroons from browning. Lightly butter the parchment. Transfer the batter into a pastry bag with a plain ½-inch/1-cm round tip (you can also use a bag without a tip). Pipe 1-inch/2½-cm rounds of the mixture onto the paper, spacing them about 1 inch/2 ½ cm apart.

Bake the macaroons for about 10 minutes, until the surfaces are dry and pale beige but they are still quite soft inside. Do not let them even begin to brown. Place the pan on a wire rack. Very carefully lift a corner of the parchment and pour a spoonful of water between the parchment and the baking sheet; the steam will help release the macaroons from the paper. Cool the macaroons for 4 minutes in their pans on a wire rack. Then carefully remove them from the paper.

MULOT'S ELEGANTLY CONTEMPO-
RARY SHOP COMMANDS THE CORNER
OF THE RUE DE TOURNON AND THE
RUE LOBINEAU, A MAGNET FOR
GOURMANDS OF THE 6TH
ARRONDISSEMENT.

FILLING: In a food processor or electric mixer, combine the almond paste, butter, and vanilla until smooth. Either pipe a small amount of filling through a pastry bag onto the flat side of a macaroon or gently spread a little filling with a small spatula or butter knife. Sandwich the flat side of a plain macaroon onto the filled one and press very gently; repeat with the remaining macaroons and filling.

MAKES ABOUT 18 FILLED
MACAROONS

Quiche aux Courgettes et Tomates

[ZUCCHINI AND TOMATO QUICHE]

PÂTE À QUICHE (QUICHE PASTRY)

1 CUP/125 G ALL-PURPOSE FLOUR

2 TABLESPOONS CORNSTARCH

¼ CUP/60 G UNSALTED BUTTER,
CUT INTO PIECES, SOFTENED

½ TEASPOON SALT

2 TABLESPOONS COLD WATER,
OR AS NEEDED

2 LARGE EGG YOLKS

FILLING

2 SMALL ZUCCHINI

2 TABLESPOONS/25 G UNSALTED
BUTTER

1 SMALL GARLIC CLOVE, MINCED

SALT

FRESHLY GROUND BLACK PEPPER

2 LARGE EGGS

1 CUP/250 ML MILK

¾ CUP/175 ML CRÈME FRAICHE
OR HEAVY CREAM

2 FRESH BASIL LEAVES,
CHOPPED, OR 1 TEASPOON DRIED

1 SPRIG FRESH CILANTRO,
CHOPPED

1 SPRIG FRESH CHERVIL,
CHOPPED, OR ¼ TEASPOON
DRIED

1 RIPE PLUM TOMATO, CORED,
SEEDED, AND CUT IN SMALL DICE

remove the paper and beans and bake until very pale gold but not yet baked through, 8 to 10 minutes longer. Remove from the oven and set aside on a rack.

FILLING: Meanwhile, rinse the zucchini, trim the ends, and slice about $1/8$ inch/$1/3$ cm thick. Blanch in boiling salted water for 3 minutes; drain immediately and refresh under cold water. Drain well.

Heat the butter in a skillet over medium heat. Add the drained zucchini and garlic and sprinkle with salt and pepper. Sauté, tossing, for 5 minutes.

In a mixing bowl, whisk together the eggs, milk, cream, basil, cilantro, chervil, and salt and pepper to taste. Scatter the zucchini mixture over the pastry shell. Scatter the tomato over the zucchini. Place the pan on the center oven rack and gently pour the egg mixture into the pastry shell.

Bake until the custard has just set and is lightly golden, about 30 minutes. Carefully remove the sides of the pan and cool the quiche briefly on a wire rack. Serve warm.

MAKES ONE 9-INCH/23-CM QUICHE

❋

Brioches aux Gouttes de Chocolat

. . . .

[CHOCOLATE CHIP BRIOCHES]

. . . .

A specialty of Gérard Mulot, these pastries are wonderful as a breakfast treat, or with tea in the afternoon.

PÂTE BRIOCHE (BRIOCHE DOUGH)

2 TABLESPOONS LUKEWARM WATER

2 TEASPOONS (ABOUT $3/4$ ENVELOPE) DRY YEAST

4 CUPS/500 G SIFTED ALL-PURPOSE FLOUR

$1/4$ CUP/50 G SUGAR

$1 1/2$ TEASPOONS SALT

5 LARGE EGGS

$1 1/2$ CUPS (3 STICKS)/350 G UNSALTED BUTTER, SOFTENED

. . . .

A SLICE OF THE QUICHE AUX COURGETTES ET TOMATES REVEALS VIBRANT FRESH SLICES OF ZUCCHINI AND TOMATO LAYERED THROUGH THE CREAMY CUSTARD.

. . . .

PÂTE À QUICHE (QUICHE PASTRY): In a food processor or mixing bowl, combine the flour, cornstarch, and butter until crumbly. Dissolve the salt in the water; add this to the flour mixture with the egg yolks and mix just until the dough comes together. Wrap in plastic and chill at least 1 hour.

Roll out the pastry on a lightly floured surface to an 11-inch/28-cm circle about $1/8$ inch/$1/3$ cm thick. Fit the dough without stretching into a buttered 9- or $9 1/2$-inch/23- or 24-cm tart pan with a removable bottom. Chill, uncovered, at least $1/2$ hour.

Preheat the oven to 400°F./200°C. Place the pastry shell on a baking sheet; line the shell with parchment paper or lightly buttered aluminum foil and fill with dried beans, rice, or pie weights. Bake until the sides have set, about 10 minutes. Carefully

THE RICH, UNUSUAL BRIOCHES AUX GOUTTES DE CHOCOLAT, CHOCOLATE-CHIP BRIOCHES DEVELOPED BY GÉRARD MULOT, ARE A FAVORITE AMONG NEIGHBORHOOD CHILDREN FOR THEIR GOÛTER, OR AFTER-SCHOOL SNACK.

. . . .

CRÈME PÂTISSIÈRE (PASTRY CREAM)

1 CUP/250 ML MILK

½ VANILLA BEAN, SPLIT LENGTHWISE, OR 1 TEASPOON VANILLA EXTRACT

3 LARGE EGG YOLKS

¼ CUP/50 G SUGAR

2 TABLESPOONS CORNSTARCH

. . . .

ASSEMBLY

4 OUNCES/120 G CHOPPED SEMISWEET CHOCOLATE OR SEMISWEET CHOCOLATE CHIPS

1 LARGE EGG, WELL BEATEN, FOR GLAZE

PÂTE À BRIOCHE (BRIOCHE DOUGH): Place the lukewarm water in a measuring cup and sprinkle with the yeast. Let stand for 10 minutes, then transfer to the bowl of an electric mixer fitted with a dough hook or a large mixing bowl. Add the sifted flour, sugar, salt, and 3 eggs. Mix at low speed until blended, using the dough hook or by hand with a wooden spoon. Gradually add the remaining 2 eggs and raise the speed to medium. Mix until the dough is smooth, elastic, and fairly soft, about 10 minutes. When it is ready, it should stick to the sides and bottom of the bowl.

Gradually add the butter 2 tablespoons at a time, mixing just until it has been absorbed, then quickly adding more. Don't overmix, or the dough will become warm. Transfer the dough to a buttered plastic container or mixing bowl, cover with plastic wrap, and set aside in a warm, draft-free place until the dough has doubled in volume, 1½ to 2 hours. Punch down or fold the dough over onto itself. Cover again with plastic wrap and refrigerate overnight.

CRÈME PÂTISSIÈRE (PASTRY CREAM): Bring the milk and vanilla bean to a boil over medium-high heat in a heavy saucepan. In a large nonaluminum mixing bowl, whisk the egg yolks and sugar, then add the cornstarch and whisk until well blended. Gradually pour the hot milk into the egg mixture, whisking constantly, then return the mixture to the saucepan and bring to a boil. Boil over medium-high heat, whisking vigorously, for 2 minutes. Strain the cream into a clean mixing bowl; if you are using vanilla extract, add it now. Place a sheet of plastic wrap directly onto the surface of the custard. Cool, then chill at least 1 hour, and up to 3 days.

ASSEMBLY: Roll out the cold dough on a lightly floured work surface to a 12 x 18-inch/30 x 45-cm rectangle, about ⅛ inch/⅓ cm thick. Stir the cold pastry cream once or twice to smooth it. With a spatula, spread 1 cup/250 ml of the pastry cream over the surface in a thin layer, reserving the rest for another use. Scatter the chocolate pieces or chips over the surface. Fold the short ends of the rectangle toward the middle, so one short end meets the other in the center.

With a very sharp knife, cut the dough in half along the center seam. Cut each half crosswise in 12 strips, cutting decisively all the way through so the dough doesn't pull. Place the strips on a baking sheet lined with parchment paper, spacing them about ¾ inch/2 cm apart. Cover loosely with plastic wrap and let rise until the dough is puffy, about 1½ hours.

Preheat the oven to 375°F./190°C. Lightly brush the tops of the dough strips with the beaten egg. Bake until golden brown, about 20 minutes. Cool the brioches completely in the pan on a wire rack.

MAKES 24 PASTRIES

MULOT'S MACARONS IN VANILLA, CHOCOLATE, STRAWBERRY, COFFEE, AND PISTACHIO ARE PURE INDULGENCE.

VOLUPTUOUS RANKS OF MERINGUES CHANTILLY COMMAND THE DISPLAY CASE OF AU PÉCHÉ MIGNON.

Meringues Géantes · Meringues Chantilly

Flan Grand-Mère · Religieuses

Tarte Nougat-Pommes

Tuiles aux Amandes

The cheerful peach facade of Au Péché Mignon stands out as distinctly from its surroundings as a pansy blooming through a crack in a flagstone walk. Set along the avenue Pierre Larousse, a low-rise, commercial thoroughfare in the suburb of Malakoff, just one minute away from Paris, Au Péché Mignon is a sign of new life in this old proletarian neighborhood. The shop was acquired in the late 1980s by two young, ambitious former restaurant chefs, Jean-Michel Noël and Henri Grenier, both in their twenties when they moved in. There has been a *pâtisserie* on the site for more than half a century, but everything about today's Au Péché Mignon is fresh and vital, from the airy pastel decor to the tempting and generously proportioned *pâtisseries*. From 6:30 in the morning on, the shop's windows are luminous with the golden glow of puffy, just-baked croissants, airy *chaussons aux pommes*—apple puff pastries—rustic, eggy flans, and sensuous, cream-filled éclairs.

Unlike other, more celebrated *pâtissiers* who work with large teams of assistants, Jean-Michel and Henri produce all their *pâtisseries* themselves, with the occasional help of two part-time apprentices. This means days that begin at 3:30 A.M. and extend past 8:00 P.M., and nights that include only four hours of sleep. "It's tough," confides the lushly bearded Henri. "You think you'll get used to it, but you never do. Even after four or five years of the same schedule, getting up at three in the morning never feels natural." While Henri and Jean-

STANDING BEFORE THE PALE PEACH FACADE OF THEIR YOUNG PÂTISSERIE ARE (LEFT TO RIGHT) OWNERS JEAN-MICHEL NOËL AND HENRI GRENIER, AND JEAN-MICHEL'S SISTER, CATHERINE.

Michel toil in the tiny, old-fashioned kitchen, heavy with the aromas of caramelized sugar, creamed butter, and melted chocolate, Jean-Michel's sister, Catherine, manages the front of the shop, greeting the familiar customers and wrapping their carefully selected confections in neat, lime-green paper packages. The neighborhood clientele now includes a smattering of artists and photographers among the aging, working-class population that once defined Malakoff, still a stronghold of the French communist party.

Among the busiest times of the week at Au Péché Mignon are Sundays just after morning mass, when parishioners from the Catholic church directly across the street stream in to pick up a special dessert for Sunday dinner or afternoon tea. After a taste of the Eucharist, the rich pastries must seem decidedly

decadent, an impression that may well have originally inspired this *pâtisserie's* playful name. *Un péché mignon* means, literally, "a little (forgivable) sin," or, more figuratively, "a particular weakness." The shop is aptly named. One glimpse of these delectable treats will lure even the most abstemious into the *péché mignon* of joyful indulgence.

✽

Meringues Géantes

....

These are indeed giant meringues—larger than a softball—crisp outside and soft and puffy within.

1 CUP/250 ML EGG WHITES
(ABOUT 8 LARGE)

1 CUP/200 G GRANULATED SUGAR

2 CUPS/285 G CONFECTIONERS'
SUGAR

½ CUP/40 G SLICED BLANCHED
ALMONDS

Preheat the oven to 200°F./100°C. Line 2 baking sheets with lightly buttered parchment paper, buttered-side up. Beat the egg whites with an electric mixer at medium speed until they begin to form soft peaks. Gradually add the granulated sugar, beating until the whites are stiff but not dry. Place the confectioners' sugar on a sheet of parchment or wax paper. Add it to the meringue in a thin stream, gently folding it in with a rubber spatula.

With a skimmer or large serving spoon, form the meringue mixture into 5 large balls on the baking sheets, building them about 3 inches high and spacing them about ¾ inch/2 cm apart. Sprinkle with the sliced almonds.

Bake for 1 ½ to 2 hours, with the handle of a wooden spoon holding the oven door slightly ajar. Watch carefully as the meringues bake; they should color to a pale beige and be crisp on the outside but slightly soft within. If the meringues are coloring too quickly, lower the oven heat slightly. Cool the meringues on the baking sheet on a wire rack.

MAKES 5 GIANT MERINGUES

❀

Meringues Chantilly
....

These meringues are smaller and crisper than the *Meringues Géantes.* They are sandwiched with *crème Chantilly,* or sweetened vanilla-flavored whipped cream.

1 RECIPE MERINGUES GÉANTES (ABOVE)

....

CRÈME CHANTILLY (WHIPPED CREAM)

1 CUP/250 ML HEAVY CREAM, WELL CHILLED

3½ TABLESPOONS/50 G SUGAR

½ VANILLA BEAN, SPLIT LENGTH-WISE, OR 1 ½ TEASPOONS VANILLA EXTRACT

Preheat the oven to 200°F./100°C. Prepare the meringue mixture as directed in the recipe above, spooning or piping them through a pastry bag into 16 smaller mounds onto a sheet of greased parchment paper placed on a baking sheet. Each meringue should be about 2½ inches wide, spaced about ¾ inch/2 cm apart.

Bake for 1½ to 1¾ hours, with the handle of a wooden spoon holding the oven door slightly ajar. The meringues should still be very pale and fairly crisp. Remove from the baking sheet and cool on a wire rack.

CRÈME CHANTILLY (WHIPPED CREAM): Place the cream in a mixing bowl with the sugar. Scrape the seeds from the vanilla pod into the cream or add the vanilla extract. Beat or whisk just until the cream forms soft peaks. Transfer the cream to a pastry bag with a large star tip, about 1½ inches/3 cm.

Pipe the cream on the flat side of one meringue, finishing with a wavy

flourish. Gently place a second meringue on top, forming a "sandwich," then set the meringues on their sides, so that there are meringues left and right with cream in the center, rather than in a traditional sandwich arrangement with meringues top and bottom. Refrigerate 1 hour before serving. These meringues should be served within a few hours of preparing so that they do not get soggy.

MAKES ABOUT 8 FILLED MERINGUES

❀

Flan Grand-Mère
....

You can make this rustic flan tart with either puff pastry, as it is at Au Péché Mignon, or with *pâte sucrée.* If you use purchased puff pastry, try to find a brand that is made with butter.

½ RECIPE PUFF PASTRY (PAGE 116), REFRIGERATED OVERNIGHT, OR USE PATE SUCRÉE (PAGE 123), CHILLED 1 HOUR

....

CUSTARD FILLING

¼ CUP/60 ML WATER

1 QUART/1 L MILK

1 VANILLA BEAN, SPLIT LENGTH-WISE, OR 1 TABLESPOON VANILLA EXTRACT

¾ CUP PLUS 2 TABLESPOONS/ 175 G SUGAR

¼ CUP/25 G GROUND BLANCHED ALMONDS

¼ CUP PLUS 2 TABLESPOONS/ 60 G POTATO STARCH OR CORNSTARCH

8 LARGE EGGS

6 LARGE EGG YOLKS

⅓ CUP/50 G CONFECTIONERS' SUGAR, FOR GLAZE (OPTIONAL)

Butter a 9- or 10-inch/23- or 25-cm tart pan with high sides, or an 8- or 9-inch/20- or 23-cm springform pan. Roll out the pastry on a lightly floured work surface to an 11-inch/28-cm circle with a thickness of about ⅛ inch/⅓ cm. Fit the pastry without stretching into the pan, trimming it flush with the edges of the tart pan or forming an even edge about 1¾ inches/4 cm high in the springform pan. Patch any cracks

....

MERINGUES GÉANTES, FLAVORED WITH ALMONDS AND LIGHT AS AIR, SEEM TO FLOAT LIKE CUMULUS CLOUDS ABOVE THE COUNTERTOP.

A COUNTRY GRANDMOTHER'S RECIPE INSPIRED JEAN-MICHEL NOËL AND HENRI GRENIER'S LUSCIOUS FLAN GRAND-MÈRE.

with the trimmings of the dough. Chill the pastry, uncovered, for ½ hour.

Preheat the oven to 375°F./190°C. Place the pastry shell on a jelly roll pan, which helps to catch the butter expelled by the crust, or on a baking sheet; line it with parchment paper or lightly buttered aluminum foil, buttered-side down, and fill with dried beans or rice. Bake until the sides have set, about 15 minutes. Carefully remove the foil and bake 5 minutes longer, or until the bottom of the pastry is pale gold. Remove from the oven.

CUSTARD FILLING: Meanwhile, bring the water to a boil over medium-high heat in a large heavy nonaluminum saucepan (this will prevent the milk from scorching). Add the milk and vanilla bean and bring to a boil. In a large nonaluminum mixing bowl, whisk the sugar, ground almonds, and potato starch or cornstarch until free of lumps. Add the eggs and egg yolks and whisk until well blended. Gradually pour about half of the hot milk into the mixing bowl, whisking, then return to the saucepan and bring to a boil, whisking constantly. Boil, whisking vigorously, for 1 minute. Strain the cream into a large mixing bowl. If you are using vanilla extract, add it now.

Pour the custard into the prebaked shell until the shell is just full (you will probably have a little extra) and bake until the filling is puffed slightly and lightly golden, 45 to 50 minutes. Place the pan on a wire rack and cool for 30 minutes. Carefully remove the sides of the pan. Refrigerate the tart, loosely covered.

The tart is ready to serve as it is, but if you like, the top can be glazed before serving as it is at Au Péché Mignon: Preheat the broiler for 5 minutes, until very hot. Sprinkle the confectioners' sugar over the surface of the custard and caramelize under the broiler just until lightly browned.

MAKES 8 SERVINGS

Religieuses

This is a classic French pastry supposedly modeled after the shape of old-fashioned nuns, for whom this variation on the éclair was named. A large cream-filled puff is glazed with fondant, then topped with a smaller cream-filled and glazed puff. You can flavor the filling and glaze with coffee or chocolate, or make some of each. This recipe is for making a batch of assorted chocolate- and coffee-flavored *Religieuses*. Fill the puffs as close to serving time as possible so the *choux* pastry doesn't get soggy.

1 RECIPE PÂTE À CHOUX (CREAM PUFF PASTE), AT ROOM TEMPERATURE (PAGE 147)

1 EGG, BEATEN, FOR GLAZE

FILLING

1 RECIPE (ABOUT 3 CUPS/750 ML) CRÈME PÂTISSIÈRE (PASTRY CREAM; RECIPE FOLLOWS)

1 TABLESPOON INSTANT COFFEE, PREFERABLY ESPRESSO OR OTHER DARK ROAST, MIXED WITH 2 TEASPOONS HOT WATER

2 OUNCES/60 G SEMISWEET CHOCOLATE, CUT UP AND MELTED OVER A DOUBLE BOILER

FONDANT GLAZE

8 OUNCES (2/3 CUP)/250 G FONDANT (SEE MAIL-ORDER SOURCES, PAGE 156)

2 TEASPOONS INSTANT COFFEE, PREFERABLY ESPRESSO OR OTHER DARK ROAST, MIXED WITH 1½ TEASPOONS HOT WATER

2 OUNCES/60 G SEMISWEET CHOCOLATE, CUT UP AND MELTED OVER A DOUBLE BOILER

SYRUP (IF NEEDED)

¼ CUP/60 G SUGAR

⅓ CUP/70 ML WATER

Prepare the *pâte à choux* and let it rest in a bowl covered with plastic wrap for 1 hour.

Preheat the oven to 425°F./220°C. Line a baking sheet with parchment paper, or butter and flour the baking sheet.

Fit a pastry bag with a ⅝-inch/1½-cm plain tip. Spoon the *pâte à choux* into the bag and gently press it down into the bottom of the bag. Holding the bag at a 45-degree angle to the pan, with the tip touching the paper, form 8 to 10 puffs about 2 inches/5 cm wide and 8 to 10 puffs about 1 inch/2½ cm wide, which will serve as the "heads." Space the puffs about 1 inch/2½ cm apart; lift the tip of the pastry bag as each puff is formed. If it makes it easier, you can trace circles on the paper with a pencil to guide you. Brush the puffs with the beaten egg.

Bake for 10 minutes, or until the puffs have risen and are beginning to color. Lower the oven to 350°F./175°C. and continue to bake until the puffs are golden and dry, about 20 minutes longer. Cool the pan on a wire rack.

FILLING: Prepare the pastry cream. While it is still hot, divide it in half. Add about 1 tablespoon of the coffee mixture to one-half of the pastry cream; add the melted chocolate to the other.

Place the coffee-flavored pastry cream in a pastry bag with a small plain tip. Poke a hole in the bottoms of the puffs. Fill half of the large and half of the small puffs with the coffee pastry cream. You will feel when they are full by the weight. Place the chocolate pastry cream in another pastry bag with a small plain tip ½ inch/1 cm or 1 inch/2½ cm and fill the remaining puffs.

FONDANT GLAZE: For coffee fondant, heat half of the fondant in a double boiler or in a metal bowl set over simmering water. Stir in about 1 teaspoon of the coffee mixture until well combined. The fondant should be smooth and fluid. If it is too stiff, add a little syrup, made by bringing the sugar and water to a boil over medium-high heat, stirring until the sugar has dissolved. Keep the fondant over simmering water while you are working with it.

For chocolate fondant, heat half of the fondant in a double boiler or in a metal bowl set over simmering water. Stir in the melted chocolate until well combined. The fondant should be smooth and fluid. If it is too stiff, add a little syrup.

Dip the tops of the large coffee-filled puffs in the coffee fondant, letting the excess drip off. Run your index finger around the edges of the fondant to smooth the edges. Dip the top of a smaller coffee-filled puff into the coffee fondant, and place the small puff atop the larger one, attaching it while the fondant is still warm. Repeat with the remaining puffs; then glaze and assemble the chocolate-filled puffs with the chocolate fondant. Refrigerate at least 10 minutes before serving. The fresher they are the better, so serve as soon as possible after preparing, ideally within 4 hours of filling the *choux*.

MAKES 8 TO 10 PASTRIES

Éclair variation: The recipe for preparing éclairs—which in French literally means "lightning bolt"—is virtually identical to that for the *Religieuses*, except for the shape you pipe the *choux* pastry into. To pipe the éclairs, hold the bag at a 45-degree angle to the paper-lined baking sheet, with the tip touching the paper, and form about 15 parallel diagonal strips about 4 inches/10 cm long, lifting the tip of the pastry bag as you get to the end. Space the strips about 2 inches/5 cm apart. Brush with the beaten egg, then trace a pattern along the length of the éclairs with the tines of a fork. Proceed as for *Religieuses*.

....

VARIATIONS ON A THEME: BOTH THE ÉCLAIRS AND THE RELIGIEUSES IN CHOCOLATE AND COFFEE ARE CREATED FROM CHOUX PASTRY AND FLAVORED CRÈME PÂTISSIÈRE.

CRÈME PÂTISSIÈRE

....

[PASTRY CREAM]

....

This is the basic *crème pâtissière*, or cooked custard. It is used to fill éclairs, cream puffs, fruit tarts, and many other pastries.

2 CUPS/500 ML MILK

1/2 VANILLA BEAN, SPLIT LENGTHWISE, OR 1 1/2 TEASPOONS VANILLA EXTRACT

1/2 CUP/100 G SUGAR

5 LARGE EGG YOLKS

3 TABLESPOONS ALL-PURPOSE FLOUR

3 TABLESPOONS CORNSTARCH

UNSALTED BUTTER, IF DESIRED

Combine the milk, the vanilla bean, and about half of the sugar in a large nonaluminum casserole or wide saucepan over medium heat and bring to a boil. Meanwhile, in a nonaluminum mixing bowl, whisk the egg yolks with the remaining sugar or beat in an electric mixer until they are pale and form a ribbon when dropped from the whisk or beater, about 5 minutes. Sift the flour and cornstarch into the egg yolk mixture and mix gently until blended.

Gradually pour the hot milk mixture into the egg yolk mixture, stirring, then return to the saucepan and bring to a boil over medium heat, stirring constantly. Boil, whisk-

THROUGHOUT THE DAY, THE WINDOWS OF AU PÉCHÉ MIGNON ARE GOLDEN
WITH THE GLOW OF JUST-BAKED PASTRIES, WHICH HERE INCLUDE A VARIETY
OF BRIOCHES AND CHAUSSONS AUX POMMES, APPLE PUFF-PASTRIES.

Tarte Nougat-Pommes

....

[NOUGAT-APPLE TART]

....

This rustic apple tart, a favorite at
Au Péché Mignon, has a delicious
crunchy almond topping.

¹/₂ RECIPE PUFF PASTRY
(PAGE 116), CHILLED OVERNIGHT
(OR USE PATE SUCRÉE, CHILLED
1 HOUR, PAGE 28)

5 GOLDEN DELICIOUS APPLES

¹/₂ LEMON

4 TABLESPOONS (¹/₂ STICK)/
60 G UNSALTED BUTTER, CUT UP

4 TABLESPOONS/60 G SUGAR

....

NOUGAT

1¹/₄ CUPS PLUS 2 TABLE-
SPOONS/100 G SLICED ALMONDS

¹/₄ CUP PLUS 3 TABLESPOONS/
100 G SUGAR

3 LARGE EGG WHITES

Butter a 10 ¹/₂-inch/27-cm tart pan
with high sides or an 8- or 9-inch/
20- or 23-cm springform pan. Roll
out the pastry on a lightly floured
work surface to an 11-inch/28-cm
circle with a thickness of about ¹/₈
inch/¹/₃ cm. Fit the pastry without
stretching into the pan, trimming it
flush with the edges of the tart pan or
forming an even edge about 1¹/₂ inch-
es/4 cm high in the springform pan.
Chill the pastry for ¹/₂ hour.

Preheat the oven to 375°F./190°C.
Place the pastry shell in a jelly roll
pan, which helps catch the butter
expelled by the crust, or on a baking
sheet; line the shell with lightly buttered parchment paper or aluminum
foil, buttered-side down, and fill with
dried beans or rice. Bake for 20 minutes, or until the pastry is pale gold.
Remove from the oven and carefully
remove the weights and paper.

While the pastry is baking, peel
the apples and rub them with the cut
side of the lemon to prevent darken-
ing. Halve the apples, remove the
cores, and cut each half in 8 wedges.

ing vigorously, for 2 minutes. Strain
the cream into a mixing bowl; if you
are using vanilla extract, add it now.
Dot the surface with butter, if
desired, or lay a sheet of plastic wrap
directly on the cream to prevent the
formation of a skin. Cool the pastry
cream on a wire rack, then refrigerate until needed. The cream can be
kept, covered and refrigerated, for 2
or 3 days.

MAKES ABOUT 2³/₄ CUPS/675 ML

PÂTE À CHOUX

....

[CREAM PUFF PASTE]

....

This is the basic pastry used for
cream puffs and éclairs and it is one
of the easiest pastries to make in the
entire *pâtisserie* repertoire.

1 CUP/250 ML WATER

1 CUP/250 ML MILK

1 TEASPOON SALT

1 TEASPOON SUGAR

⁷/₈ CUP (1³/₄ STICKS)/200 G
UNSALTED BUTTER, CUT IN
PIECES

1²/₃ CUPS/235 G ALL-PURPOSE
FLOUR

6 TO 7 LARGE EGGS

Preheat the oven to 425°F./220°C. In
a large heavy saucepan, combine the
water, milk, salt, sugar, and butter.
Bring to a boil over medium-high
heat, stirring until the butter melts
and the liquid is boiling.

Meanwhile, sift the flour onto a
sheet of wax paper. Remove the pan
from the heat and add the flour in a
thin stream, stirring vigorously with
a wooden spoon. Return the pan to
medium heat and stir vigorously for
1 minute, until the mixture pulls
away from the side of the pan. This
will dry the mixture out. Don't over-
cook at this stage.

Transfer the mixture to the bowl
of an electric mixer (or continue to
mix with a wooden spoon). Working
at medium speed, incorporate the
eggs one at a time, mixing until the
dough is nicely smooth. After the
fifth egg, beat the last 2 individually,
adding just as much as you need so
that when the mixture is lifted with
a spoon, a peak stands up, then
droops over slightly.

The unbaked dough will keep
well for 3 days, tightly sealed in the
refrigerator. It can also be successful-
ly frozen.

MAKES ABOUT 5 CUPS/1 L 250 ML

Nougat pommes
83ᶠ.oo

THE TARTE NOUGAT-POMMES GETS ITS UNUSUAL CRUNCH FROM A CARAMELIZED TOP OF SLICED ALMONDS.

Heat a large skillet over medium-high heat. Working in 2 or 3 batches, add some of the butter (you may need less if the skillet is nonstick), then some of the apples. Cook the apples, tossing occasionally, until lightly golden, about 3 minutes. Add some of the sugar and cook, tossing, for 1 minute longer. Transfer the apples to a plate with a slotted spoon and repeat until all of the apples have been cooked until tender but still hold their shape. If there are juices left in the pan, boil them down to a spoonful or two. Spread the apples evenly into the tart shell and pour the juices over.

NOUGAT: Combine the sliced almonds, sugar, and egg whites in a mixing bowl. Stir to combine the ingredients without beating the whites. Pour the nougat mixture over the apples and bake the tart for 35 to 40 minutes, or until the nougat is lightly golden and crusty. Cool the tart on a wire rack and serve at room temperature.

MAKES 6 TO 8 SERVINGS

....

AU PÉCHÉ MIGNON'S OVERSIZED TUILES, OR TILE COOKIES, GET THEIR SHAPE FROM BEING DRAPED OVER BORDEAUX WINE BOTTLES.

Tuiles aux Amandes

....

[ALMOND TILE COOKIES]

....

If you don't want to bake all the cookies at once, the unbaked batter will keep about a week, tightly sealed in the refrigerator. Stir well before using.

2 CUPS/180 G SLICED BLANCHED ALMONDS

1 ⅓ CUP/240 G SUGAR

6 LARGE EGG WHITES

1 TEASPOON VANILLA EXTRACT

6 TABLESPOONS ALL-PURPOSE FLOUR

4 TABLESPOONS (½ STICK)/ 60 G UNSALTED BUTTER, MELTED AND COOLED

In a large mixing bowl, stir together the almonds and sugar with a wooden spoon. Add the egg whites and vanilla, stirring to blend. Sift the flour onto a sheet of wax paper or parchment paper and add it to the bowl in a thin stream. Stir in the melted butter until blended. Cover the batter and refrigerate for at least 1 hour, or overnight.

Preheat the oven to 375°F./190°C. Butter 2 baking sheets. Drop the mixture onto the sheet, using about 2 ½ tablespoons for each cookie and spacing them about 5 inches/12 cm apart. With a metal spatula or a fork dipped in cold water, gently pat each mound of dough as thin as possible. Bake until lightly golden at the edges and pale in the centers, about 8 minutes. Cool the pan on top of the stove or on a wire rack for about 3 minutes to allow the cookies to set. With a thin spatula, very carefully remove them from the baking sheet, loosening the edges first, and gently drape them over a wine bottle or a straight-sided glass so they curl gently. (If the cookies become too cool to curl easily, return the sheet to the turned-off oven for 30 seconds, just until they are warm enough to be flexible.) Cool the cookies completely.

MAKES ABOUT SIX 6-INCH/ 15-CM COOKIES

COMPANIES SUCH AS A. SIMON IN PARIS, WHERE THE GOODS ABOVE ARE STOCKED, SUPPLY A PANOPLY OF BAKEWARE.

Being equipped with the proper tools makes the practice of any art or craft easier and more efficient. In specialized baking—creating French *pâtisserie* and traditional breads, for example—this is especially true. Many items in the French baker's arsenal have been designed specifically for the preparation of one particular pastry or bread, notably the wide range of baking pans and molds. A madeleine in a cupcake tin simply is not a madeleine. The delicate, fluted scallop shell form of this little cake that triggered Proust's transcendental experience is essential to its identity. A *financier* in any other mold—a ramekin, for example—would taste as sweet . . . but it wouldn't be a *financier*, a small, rectangular cake said to resemble a brick of gold bullion. Most of the recipes in this book can be prepared with a bare minimum of equipment—a rolling pin, a cutting board, a whisk, a few mixing bowls, a tart pan, some cake pans, a wire cooling rack, a loaf pan, a couple of saucepans, a baking sheet, a cupcake tin, and a spatula—things an ordinary kitchen would usually contain. But the more specialized the baking equipment you have, the more authentic the baked goods you produce will be. What follows is a descriptive listing of some of the traditional French tools and equipment that facilitate the creation of the pastries and breads in this book. They are available both from U.S. mail-order sources and from Paris restaurant supply houses, all listed in the Directory following this chapter.

WORK SURFACES: a *marble pastry slab,* about 2 feet/60 cm square, or slightly smaller. Keeps dough cool during rolling out; can be chilled when working in a warm environment. (An ideal kitchen temperature for pastry making is just under 60°F./30°C. A *large butcher block cutting board,* also about 2 feet square, for mixing and kneading bread doughs, which respond best to a warmer environment, around 72°F./40°C.

MIXING BOWLS: an assortment of *stainless steel bowls* in a variety of sizes, especially useful for heating over simmering or hot water; a large *copper bowl* for whisking egg whites; two or three *earthenware* and *ceramic bowls,* pleasant to work with and practical for a variety of mixing and dough-rising needs.

ROLLING PINS: a *marble* or *steel rolling pin* for rolling out pastry dough; one of hardwood, with traditional handles, or a French-style *rouleau,* a long, sleek cylinder with no handles; a *tutové,* a heavy, hardwood rolling pin covered with a sheath of ribbed plastic designed for rolling out *pâte feuilletée,* or puff pastry (all but the final turn, that is, which is done with a conventional rolling pin).

TIME-WORN ANTIQUE BAKEWARE, SUCH AS THESE PIECES STILL USED
IN THE KITCHENS OF AU PÉCHÉ MIGNON, IS JUST AS PRACTICAL AS—BUT
BETTER SEASONED THAN—NEW BAKEWARE.

. . . .

MIXING AND SCRAPING TOOLS: at least three—small, medium, and large—*sturdy wire whisks;* five or six *hardwood wooden mixing spoons;* two or three *rubber spatulas* in varying sizes; a *pastry corne,* a wedgelike spatula without a handle, usually of hard plastic or nylon (antique ones of animal horn can still be found); *dough scraper* or *dough knife,* a multipurpose steel blade with a long wooden or plastic handle across the top, used by Paris bakers for a variety of tasks—stirring, scraping, creaming, and dough cutting.

KNIVES: a *bread* knife, a sharp, serrated or scalloped-edge knife with a wooden handle and a generous blade about a foot long for slicing cleanly through fresh, crusty breads; a *palette* knife, or ideally two of these metal spatulas with rounded tips, a short one about 6 inches/15 cm long for decorating cakes and another about 10 inches/25 cm long for spreading batters and fillings, smoothing frosting, and lifting pastries; a short, sharp *paring knife;* a top-quality, very sharp chef's knife, of carbon-steel or high-carbon steel about 10 inches/25 cm long for innumerable kitchen tasks, including slicing and chopping, accompanied by a good sharpening steel; a pastry wheel, a sharp little wheel on a stick, for cutting and marking dough; a *lame,* a small, razorlike knife to slit the top of a bread loaf before baking (a single-edge razor from an art supply shop works well, too).

PASTRY BAGS AND BRUSHES: two canvas or nylon *pastry bags* with a variety of *metal tubes* with plain or star tips to fit within for piping toppings, fillings, or batters; two or three flat *pastry brushes* in varying widths, with wooden handles and natural bristles for glazing tarts, coating molds, and brushing egg wash across pastry doughs and pans.

MOLDS AND PANS: (Except where noted, the bakeware below is available in tinned steel and sometimes in heavier-gauge black steel, which absorbs more heat, creating a browner crust more quickly—sometimes too quickly, especially for tarts and pastries where a pale crust is desirable—and which can never be washed, since water rusts its surface.) A *kugelhopf mold,* a deep fluted tube pan, ideally of earthenware, although also available in copper and tinned steel, specifically for the Alsatian coffee cake for which it is named; for *madeleines,* a pan of fluted, shell-shaped molds; for *financiers,* a pan of slope-sided rectangular-shaped molds; for *charlottes,* a deep, round slope-sided mold; *timbale molds,* like oversized thimbles, for making Max Poilâne's chocolate *bouchons* and some *babas;* a *savarin ring mold,* round and shallow with two interior indentations for another variation of the *baba; quiche* and *tart molds,* in a variety of sizes from individual 3 inches/8 cm to 14 inches/35 cm and more, with fluted sides (about $^1/_2$ inch/$^1/_4$ cm deep for individual, about 1³/₄ inches/3 cm deep for large sizes), some with false bottoms; *mini brioche molds,* small and round with deeply fluted sìdes, these little pans for *petites brioches* look like spread-out cupcake tin liners; tall, cylindrical *brioche mousseline* molds for a classic tall brioche; French-style *loaf pans,* with sloping sides, generally about 8 inches/20 cm long, for molding *pain brioché, pain de mie, pain au maïs,* and other small loaf breads as well as *le cake,* a pound cake–style loaf cake; *moules à manquer,* French layer-cake pans, in a variety of sizes, from 6 inches/15 cm to about 12 inches/30 cm in diameter, and from 1 to 3 inches deep, 2¹/₂ to 8 cm with slightly sloping sides; *flan rings,* rings of steel made in a variety of sizes, the 9¹/₂- or 11-inch/25- or 28-cm size being most practical for home use, used for molding tarts directly on a baking sheet (the rings have no bottom); *bûche* or *trough pans,* round-bottomed, U-shaped pans for baking *bûche-de-Noël* Christmas log cakes, as well as *coulibiacs* and other *entrées en croûte;* and *tartelette* and *barquette* molds, tiny round or boat-shaped molds with pointed ends for making hors d'oeuvres or bite-sized tarts; *baguette pans,* two- to six-loaf molded pans for forming long, narrow loaves in individual channels or "troughs" pressed into the pan; *couches,* a long, channeled arrangement of wood and canvas to help long strips of baguette dough, destined to bake on a sheet or on the oven floor rather than in a mold, retain their baguette form during their final rising; *bannetons,* round or long and narrow wicker baskets with heavy linen liners stitched in, used by bakers to form and hold dough during the final rising.

BAKING SHEETS: In the *boulangeries* and *pâtisseries* of Paris, the classic baking sheet is a *large, heavy-gauge black steel rectangle* with shallow sloping sides, excellent for baking breads, cookies, sheet cakes, and as a base for tart molds or flan rings, if the crust can get rather dark. It does a yeoman job of retaining and distributing heat, giving breads a firm, crusty bottom. The 13 x 20-inch/33 x 51-cm and the 16 x 24-inch/40 x 61-cm sizes are the most versatile, but with a tart or two on them they can be heavy to lift. A round version of the classic baking sheet, called a *tourtière,* most commonly available in 11- and 14-inch/28- and 35-cm diameters, is lighter and more practical as a base for baking a single cake or tart.

BAKING STONES: The radiant heat characteristics of the classic French bread oven is due to its brick construction; to duplicate or at least approximate this essential baking quality in a home electric or gas oven, there are a variety of baking stones, ceramic baking tiles, and pizza stones available from several sources. Bread is baked directly on top of the stones or tiles, which are placed on the bottom rack of the oven and sprinkled with cornmeal. The baking stone can be reserved for occasional baking, or can be left in the oven, enhancing the heating properties for all baking needs.

AUTHENTIC ACCESSORIES: A *beam-balance scale,* such as those made by Terraillon, if you want to do weight measures rather than volume measures; a *pelle,* or peel, a long-handled, flat-surfaced "shovel" to transfer loaves of bread from their last rising into the oven when baking directly on the oven floor or on a baking stone, and for removing breads when they are done. Of course, unless you have a professional bread oven, you don't need a *pelle* with a 10-foot/3-m handle. There is a short, pizza-making version available that would work well at home, as would a small rectangle of wood or masonite about ¹/₂ inch/1 cm thick; a *dredge* looks like an overgrown salt shaker, about the size of a large jelly jar with a perforated screw-on top, and is very practical for dusting on confectioners' sugar or cocoa powder to finish tarts and other *pâtisseries; kitchen parchment,* a strong, greaseproof paper, is perfect for lining a baking sheet instead of greasing it, and saves on cleanup time; you can also use it instead of aluminum foil to lay over the tops of tarts and cakes if they begin to get too brown before their baking time is up; *paper doilies,* lacy paper circles, squares, or rectangles, placed underneath pastries give an authentic finishing touch when serving; most Paris *pâtisseries* use pristine white doilies, but venerable Stohrer chooses regal gold.

············

A SELECTION OF CLASSIC EARTHENWARE KUGELHOPF MOLDS ARE AMONG THE REGIONAL WARES TO BE FOUND AT AUX COEURS D'ALSACE ON THE ILE-ST.-LOUIS.

Au Péché Mignon
77-quater avenue Pierre-Larousse
Malakoff
Tel.: 42-53-44-95

....

Dalloyau
99–101 rue du Faubourg-St.-Honoré
Paris 8e
Tel.: 43-59-18-10
also
2 place Edmond-Rostand
Paris 6e
Tel.: 43-29-31-10

....

Marcel Haupois
35 rue des Deux-Ponts
Paris 4e (Ile-St.-Louis)
Tel.: 43-54-57-59

....

Ganachaud
150 rue Ménilmontant
Paris 20e
Tel.: 46-36-13-82
also
La Flûte Gana
226 rue des Pyrénées
Paris 20e
Tel.: 43-58-42-62

....

Ladurée
16 rue Royale
Paris 8e
Tel.: 42-60-21-79

....

André Lerch:
Pâtisserie-Boulangerie
Alsacienne
4 rue Cardinal-Lemoine
Paris 5e
Tel.: 43-26-15-80

....

Lenôtre
44 rue d'Auteuil
Paris 16e
Tel.: 45-24-52-52
Also many other locations,
including 49 avenue Victor Hugo,
Paris 16e, and 3 and 5 rue du
Havre, Paris 9e

....

La Maison du Chocolat
225 rue du Faubourg-St.-Honoré
Paris 8e
Tel.: 42-27-39-44
also
52 rue François-1er
Paris 8e
Tel.: 47-23-38-25

....

Moulin de la Vierge
166 avenue de Suffren
Paris 15e
Tel.: 47-83-45-55
also
105 rue Vercingétorix
Paris 14e
Tel.: 45-43-09-84

....

Gérard Mulot
76 rue de Seine
Paris 6e
Tel.: 43-26-85-77

....

Max Poilâne
87 rue Brancion
Paris 15e
Tel.: 48-28-45-90

....

Jean-Luc Poujauran
20 rue Jean-Nicot
Paris 7e
Tel.: 47-05-80-88

....

Stohrer
51 rue Montorgueil
Paris 2e
Tel.: 42-33-38-20

✳

OTHER RECOMMENDED
PÂTISSERIES AND
BOULANGERIES

Aux Délices de Sèvres:
G. Abot
70 rue de Sèvres
Paris 7e

....

Au Panetier
10 place des Petits-Pères
Paris 2e

....

Christian Constant
26 rue du Bac
Paris 7e

....

La Petite Marquise
3 place Victor-Hugo
Paris 16e

....

Pâtisserie Millet
103 rue St.-Dominique
Paris 7e

....

Peltier
66 rue de Sèvres
Paris 15e

....

Lionel Poilâne
8 rue du Cherche-Midi
Paris 6e

....

A Paris Bread Museum

The *Musée Français du Pain* is an obscure little private museum lodged above a still-operational flour mill. It is located just across the Paris line in the southeastern suburb of Charenton-le-Pont. Lovingly assembled by Jacques Lorch, a retired former executive of the flour company, the displays of bread and baking memorabilia—1,750 items—are crowded and jumbled but fascinating. Check visiting hours carefully—there aren't many of them!

Musée Français du Pain

25 bis rue Victor-Hugo
Charenton-le-Pont (enter *into* the courtyard and look to the right to find the museum entrance)
Tel.: 43-68-43-60
Metro: Charenton-Ecoles
Open: Tuesday and Thursday from 2:00 P.M. to 4:00 P.M.
Closed July and August

❋

MAIL-ORDER FOOD SPECIALTY SOURCES

For specialty flours, the following mills offer a variety of fine bread flours, organic and otherwise, by mail. Contact each for price lists, types of flour, and other information.

Arrowhead Mills
Box 866
Hereford, Texas 79045
Tel.: 806-364-0730
All flours from organically grown grains.

....

Byrd Mill Company
P.O. Box 5167
Richmond, Virginia 23220

....

Elam's Flours
Elam Mills
2125 Gardner Road
Broadview, Illinois 60153
Tel.: 708-865-1612

....

Great Valley Mills
687 Mill Road
Telford, Pennsylvania 18969
Tel.: 215-754-7800
Excellent selection of stone-ground flours.

Walnut Acres
Penns Creek, Pennsylvania 17862
Tel.: 800-433-3998 or 717-837-0601

For Sourdough Starters:
Walnut Acres
(see above)

....

Sourdoughs International
P.O. Box 1440
Cascade, Idaho 83611
Tel.: 208-382-4828
Ed Wood, a passionate sourdough collector, offers unique starters by mail, from a 150-year-old Paris bakery, an eighteenth-century Austrian bakery, the Yukon, San Francisco, and more. Starters come with directions and recipes.

For praline paste, crystallized flowers, couverture (glazing) chocolates, and vanilla beans:

Maid of Scandinavia
3244 Raleigh Avenue
Minneapolis, Minnesota 55461
Tel.: 800-328-6722 or 612-927-7966

For Valrhona bulk chocolate, fondant, Callebaut praline paste, vanilla sugar, extensive catalog of specialty foods and bakeware:

Dean & DeLuca

560 Broadway
New York, New York 10012
Tel.: 212-431-1691 (in New York)
800-221-7714 (outside of
New York City)

For domestic foie gras, *delicious pâtés, terrines, and entrées*

D'Artagnan

399 St. Paul Avenue
Jersey City, New Jersey 07306
· Tel.: 800-DARTAGNAN

For excellent crème fraîche *and* fromage blanc *as well as other specialty dairy products:*

Vermont Butter and Cheese Co.

P. O. Box 95
Websterville, Vermont 05678

....

MAIL-ORDER KITCHEN EQUIPMENT AND BAKEWARE SUPPLY HOUSES

The following companies stock a wide range of American, French, and other imported baking supplies. Contact them directly for price lists and catalogs.

Bridge Kitchenware Corp.

214 East 52nd Street
New York, New York 10022
Tel.: 212-688-4220
Copper pots and pans, molds, black
steel baking sheets

....

Dean & DeLuca

560 Broadway
New York, New York 10012
Tel.: 212-431-1691 (in New York)
800-221-7714 (outside of
New York City)
Black steel baking sheets, molds,
whisks, rolling pins

....

Charles Lamalle

36 West 25th Street, 6th floor
New York, New York 10036
Tel.: 212-242-0750
This old-time French restaurant supply house has impressive but rather jumbled stock, including earthenware *kugelhopf* molds, baguette pans, pastry bags and tubes, French palette knives, ramekins, bread baskets, and more. Catalog available.

....

Williams-Sonoma

Mail-Order Dept.
P.O. Box 7456
San Francisco, California 94120-7456
Tel.: 415-421-4242
Brioche molds, baking pans, copper
molds, bowls, marble rolling pins

....

King Arthur Flour

Baker's Catalog
Box 876
Norwich, Vermont 05055
Tel.: 800-827-6836
In addition to a panoply of specialty flours, King Arthur also offers fine baking stones, peels, lames, baguette pans, knives, and molds.

....

Paris Restaurant Supply Houses

In the following shops, which sell both retail to consumers and wholesale to restaurants and hotels around the world, you will find every piece of cooking and baking equipment you've ever heard of and innumerable others you've never even dreamed of. Don't miss stopping in to browse and buy if you're in Paris. Most places are happy to pack your purchases for you to carry home, but they will not send merchandise overseas.

A. Simon
36 rue Etienne-Marcel
Paris 2e
Tel.: 42-33-71-65
Open Monday through Saturday

. . . .

Dehillerin
18–20 rue Coquillière
Paris 1er

Tel.: 42-36-53-13
Open Monday through Saturday

. . . .

MORA et Cie
13 rue Montmartre
Paris 1er
Tel.: 45-08-19-24
Open Monday through Friday

. . . .

Verrerie des Halles
15 rue du Louvre
Paris 1er
Tel.: 42-36-86-02
Open Monday through Friday

. . . .

For hand-crafted Alsatian kugelhopf molds of glazed earthenware, photographed on page 153, pain d'épices or spice-cookie molds, and many other Alsatian specialties in a beguiling little shop on the Seine owned by Françoise Ledoux-Wernert, a lovely native of Alsace:

Aux Coeurs d'Alsace
33 quai de Bourbon
Paris 4e (Ile-St.-Louis)
Tel.: 46-33-14-03
Open Tuesday through Saturday

. . . .

For antique French bakeware, collectible food storage boxes (cookies, salt, flour), antique table linens, bibs, porcelain, Barbotine plates, old cooking tools, among a vast variety of wares in a large, attractive shop just off the rue du Faubourg-St.-Honoré, not far from Hermès and the Place de la Concorde:

Au Bain Marie
10 rue Boissy-d'Anglas
Paris 8e
Tel.: 42-66-59-74
Open Monday through Saturday
They ship internationally.